THOSE WHO MADE A DIFFERENCE 3

TERRY BOSGRA

Copyright © 2022 **Terry Bosgra**

All rights reserved. No part of this publication may be reproduced, distributed, or transmitted in any form or by any means, including photocopying, recording, or other electronic or mechanical methods, without the prior written permission of the publisher, except in the case of brief quotations embodied in critical reviews and certain other noncommercial uses permitted by copyright law. For permission requests, write to the publisher, addressed "Attention: Book Rights and Permission," at the address below.

Published in the United States of America

ISBN 978-1-956741-78-0 (SC)
ISBN 978-1-956741-79-7 (Ebook)

Terry Bosgra
222 West 6th Street
Suite 400, San Pedro, CA, 90731
www.stellarliterary.com

Order Information and Rights Permission:

Quantity sales. Special discounts might be available on quantity purchases by corporations, associations, and others. For details, contact the publisher at the address above.

For Book Rights Adaptation and other Rights Permission. Call us at toll-free 1-888-945-8513 or send us an email at admin@stellarliterary.com.

Contents

Introduction 1
About the Author 2
Russell Blaylock (400) 4
Helio Gracie (401) 5
Mike Huckabee (402) 6
Lawrence B. Jones (403) 7
Steve Hilton (404) 8
Dinesh D'Souza (405) 9
David Hume (406) 10
Keli'i Akina (407) 11
Victor Davis Hanson (408) 12
Robert Vernon (409) 13
Eric Metaxas (410) 14
Irving Copi (411) 15
Cesar Pelli (412) 16
Augustine of Hippo (413) 17
William H Parker (414) 18
Millard Dean Fuller (415) 19
Julia Child (416) 20
William Worrall Mayo (417) 21
John Dalton (418) 22
Brandon Judd (419) 23
Sabina Oster Wurmbrand (420) 24
Mark A. Morgan (421) 25
Peter Schweizer (422) 26
Laura Ingraham (423) 27
Kathy Ireland (424) 28
Lisa Boothe (425) 29
Lou Holtz (426) 30
Josh Hawley (427) 31

Harmeet Dhillon (428) 32
Debra M. Lewis (429) 33
Thomas Aquinas (430) 34
Betsy Ross (431) 35
Rick Monday (432) 36
Tom Catena (433) 37
Desiderius Erasmus (434) 38
Mark Meadows (435) 39
Condoleezza Rice (436) 40
Louise (437) 41
Ariana (438) 42
Alice Ball (439) 43
Patricia Bath (440) 44
Yvonne Clark (441) 45
Victor Orban (442) 46
Mollie Hemingway (443) 47
Alfred Vogel (444) 48
Trischa Zorn (445) 49
Mae Jemison (446) 50
Tom De Meester (447) 51
Ronald Dion DeSantis (448) 52
Richard R. Kelley (449) 53
Sarah Huckabee Sanders (450) 54
Julia Coleman (451) 55
John Fund (452) 56
Rosemary Jensen (453) 57
James H. Case (454) 58
Jimmy Stewart (455) 59
Audrey Hepburn (456) 60
David Niven (457) 61
Paul Newman (458) 62
Clark Gable (459) 63

Sissel Kyrkjebo (460)	64
Shirley Temple (461)	65
Albert L Ireland (462)	66
Kay Coles James (463)	67
Michele Bachmann (464)	68
Lowell Smith Dillingham (465)	69
Sendor Nemeth (466)	70
David Yonggi Cho (467)	71
David Warren (468)	72
John Gibson Paton (469)	73
Michael Gangloff (470)	74
Peng Shuai (471)	75
Harry Weinberg (472)	76
Rudolf Bultmann (473)	77
Karl Barth (474)	78
Gerrit Cornelis Berkouwer (475)	79
Herman Boerhaave (476)	80
Winsome Sears (477)	81
Frank E. Midkiff (478)	82
Ruddy F. Tongg (479)	83
Stanley Kennedy (480)	84
Miranda Devine (481)	85
Noah Webster (482)	86
Theo H. Davies (483)	87
Francis Mills Swanzy (484)	88
Alexander Young (485)	89
William Wrigley Jr. (486)	90
Chris Gardner (487)	91
Bruce Olson (488)	92
D. Howard Hitchcock (489)	93
Bob Dole (490)	94
Hans Wilsdorf (491)	95

Leo Terrell (492) 96
Carlos Ott (493) 97
William Penn (494) 98
Naftali Bennett (495) 99
Willard Metcalf (496) 100
Olga of Kiev also called Helga (497) 101
Yulia Tymoshenko (498) 102
Niuta Teitelbaum (499) 103
Jack Webb (500) 104
Kathy Sparks (501) 105
Kim Potter (502) 106
Nigel Rowe (503) 107
Alex Newman (504) 108
Renzo Piano (505) 109
Tim Scott (506) 110
Pete Hegseth (507) 111
Anselm of Canterbury (508) 112
Immanuel Kant (509) 113
Henry L. Deneen (510) 114
Serena Williams (511) 115
Joseph John Gurney (512) 116
Elizabeth Fry (513) 117
Rachel Campos-Duffy (514) 118
Pete Anderson (515) 119
Louis Marie Cordonnier (516) 120
Jay Adams (517) 121
John Bunyan (518) 122
C. S. Lewis (519) 123
John Owen (520) 124
Richard Baxter (521) 125
Hugo Junkers (522) 126
Christiane Amanpour (523) 127

Mary Todd Lincoln (524) ... 128
Sarah Palin (525) ... 129
Maria Sharapova (526) ... 130
Louisa May Alcott (527) ... 131
Margaret (Peggy) Garner (528) ... 132
Jessica (Jessi) Combs (529) ... 133
Elizabeth Freeman (530) ... 134
Lady Jane Grey (9-day Queen) (531) ... 135
Cai Lun (532) ... 136
William R. Dunn (533) ... 137
E. V. Hill (534) ... 138
Marie Bashkirtseff (535) ... 139
Glenn Youngkin (536) ... 140
Martha Gellhorn (537) ... 141
Jacqueline Cochran (538) ... 142
Phoebe Palmer (539) ... 143
Susan Boyle (540) ... 144
Alphabetical Volume 3 ... 145

Terrybo.com

Get artwork, pillows, gifts, home decorations, apparel, etc. of Terry's portrait at:
Terrybo.com

Design by **Lana Bo**

Introduction

Some people live a life that touches a few; others live so someone will be forever different whether unintentional or deliberate.

Sometimes by being an example, others go deliberately out of their way to improve and inspire all they contact.

My school teacher touched my life in a way that made me a different person, although I was young it affected me a lifetime.

It may be a parent, teacher, neighbor, or just a friend, that reached out to make your life better;

Some are gifted to change entire communities or nations. And in these pages, we only feature those who improved life.

This book is not intended to honor people like Hitler, Mao, Poll-Pot, Stalin, or Fidel Castro and others.

There may be disagreement about some; I know that having publicly commented on Mikhail Gorbachev in this line up, who was head of the "evil empire", but we must look at the big picture, willing to see past our own bias, and learn the whole story, we hope this book will do that.

All information in these pages have been compiled from public media such as Newspaper, Magazines, as well as personal visits of about 30 or some individuals in personal interviews, and/or visits in our home, or their home or national meetings. The purpose of this book is to inspire every reader to make a difference.

Terry Bosgra

About the Author

Terry Bosgra was born in The Kingdom of the Netherlands in 1935 and grew up in a family of 7 siblings during the cold winters when Germany occupied most of Europe and every family had to live on ration cards. For our parents it was not an easy time, but children are resilient and we came through it with few scars. There were no toy stores, meaning we became innovative and made our own from scraps we found in the fields rummaging through the trash heaps of the soldiers, we always found treasures there; for us it was more fun to make and invent our own toys.

The soldiers were everywhere, but many families lived in the country and were willing to take in an extra Jewish child.

Communication and news-media was outlawed during WW-II, therefore information about the concentration camps, was not known, and only heard rumors or listened to a secret radio in the basement. In 1945 General Eisenhower opened all the camps to the media, saying: "*I want film crews, reporters, and all media to go in first, and document these atrocities so that none of this can be denied later.* "

In Amsterdam the Jewish parents were concerned with the seriously increasing dangers; Soldiers and traitors were always on the lookout for Jewish adults & children who were destined for Hitler and his bloodthirsty minions, eager to fill the trains that were headed for Auschwitz, Dachau, Buchenwald, and any of the 1000+ concentration Camps. At the trial of Nuremberg, it was clear that there were many guilty besides the key Gestapo leaders; Evidence surfaced that Hitler told Himmler: "*it is not enough for Jews to simply die; they must die in agony.*" Few were willing to stand up to the evil forces of the Reich, all lived in fear of their own safety, the guilt rests on all of Europe, no one man can murder 6 million+ Jews. Hitler and his cronies had unchecked and absolute power.

At that time, children, as well as the parents, lived with a fear, (not of the soldiers), but more so of the traitors among us, eager to please the enemy; people in this book such as Corry ten Boom, Anne Frank, and many others became victims of such traitors.

After WW-II, I joined the Marine Corps during the Korea War but as the hostilities in Korea, and in the South Pacific were winding down, we were temporarily parked in the West Indies of the coast of Venezuela. Actually, not a bad place to serve for 3 years, I was planning to discharge there and move to Nicaragua, but dad called: (mom had MS), and said "If u want to see mom, before she dies, you better head for home." I did, see mom, and went to work driving small tours through Europe. Then tried to move to the US, but could not get in, due to an over-subscribed quota, so moved to New Zealand. There fulfilled my lifetime dream of becoming a pilot, went to flight-school and got a license; Found, and married Pamela there, who became my life partner (now longer than 60 years). We moved to California, and later to Honolulu; tried working at Pan-Am but needed more flight hours so went to work in finance; there built my own financial business with great success, after 45 years sold it, and retired at age 70; then went to work with my friend Hal in Geneva doing humanitarian relief work in the Middle East & Africa. Got active in politics and am still running a daily commentary by internet running in about 60 – 80 countries. Hal (my amazing Partner) recently died.

Wrote my first book "*Abortion the Bible & the Church*" then tried this topic; "*Those who made a difference*". Every person in here has been an inspiration to me, and I hope they are to u.

This book is volume three of "*Those who made a difference*"; each book contains a one-page story of about 200 people that have gone the extra mile to make this world a better place. All information is gleaned from the public information pages; read wisely and help join me to make our world a better place; God bless.

Terry Bosgra

Russell Blaylock (400)

Russell L, Blaylock was born on Nov.15, 1945 in the US. He completed his general surgical internship and neurosurgical residency at the Medical University of South Carolina. After that, he was clinical assistant professor of neurosurgery at the University of Mississippi Medical Center and visiting professor in the biology department at Belhaven College. He was licensed to practice Neurological Surgery in N. Carolina between May 6, 1977 and December 15, 2006, (that's 30 years in a profession that takes much precisian work, I am a recipient of two such surgeries and know how much difference it makes in our lives). In that profession he developed new treatment in certain operations such as a ventriculolymphatic shunt in the treatment of hydrocephalus, which is a condition when fluid is accumulating in the brain; Blaylock devised a shunt which can be inserted surgically below the skin and drain it in to the stomach. He retired from neurosurgical practice to devote more time to neuroscience nutritional studies and research; he authored four books on nutrition and wellness such as "Health and Nutrition Secrets that can save your life," "Natural strategies for Cancer Patients", and "Cellular and Molecular Biology of Autism Spectrum Disorders," edited by Anna Strunecka. In addition to that, he's recorded several health DVD's and audio speeches, appeared on many radio and television programs. He lectures extensively to both lay and medical audiences on nutrition related subjects. The Blaylock Wellness Report is read by over 120,000 subscribers. He is the 2004 recipient of the Integrity in Science Award granted by the Westin a Price Foundation. He is retired as a clinical assistant professor, but is still associated with the Association of American Physicians and Surgeons. He serves on the editorial staffs of numerous journals such as Surgical Neurology International, and the journal of American Physicians and Surgeons, Association of American Physicians and Surgeons. Blaylock claims the supposed toxicity of numerous substances that according to scientific consensus are safe at customary exposure levels. He states that the widely used artificial sweetener aspartame is toxic and may be the cause of multiple sclerosis. He has cautioned against heavy use of artificial sweetener Splenda (sucralose). These positions are not supported by scientific consensus or regulatory bodies, as extensive studies support the safety of aspartame, sucralose and MSG. He is the author and co-author of two case reports in the journal of Neurosurgery, and has written for, and been on the editorial board, of the journal of the politically conservative non-profit organization Association of American Physicians and Surgeons. Regardless of what the medical consensus or opinions may be, in our family he is often considered the final word on health-related issues.

Helio Gracie (401)

Helio Gracie was born on October 1, 1913 in Belem, Brazil. He grew up training with his brothers and learned Judo under Sumiyuki Kotani and Argentinian Judo pioneer Chugo Sato; and also trained under Hiraichi Tada, although it is not known where most of his techniques in the Martial Arts came from. Gracie realized that he knew them theoretically; but soon began to realize that these moves were much harder to execute. Consequently, he began adapting Mitsuyo Maeda's brand of judo, already heavily based around newaza ground fighting techniques, for his smaller physique, and from these experiments, Gracie Ju-Jitsu was created. Like its parent style of judo, these techniques allowed smaller and weaker practitioners the capability to defend themselves and even defeat much larger opponents. Carlos and Helio Gracie brought a fresh eye to jiu-jitsu just as their fellow countryman had done to soccer. Gracie began his professional career at age 18 against boxer Antonio Portugal, and won that fight by submission in a short time probably an armlock in 40 seconds. His second match in that same year was in a jiu-jitsu exhibition against Takashi Namiki in September. Namiki had a 7kg (15 lb) weight advantage and was a native of Japan, just like the art of jiu-jitsu; he was expected to defeat Helio. Namiki dominated the match but Gracie wasn't defeated, leading to a draw after several rounds. Then in 1932 Gracie faced professional wrestler Fred Ebert, who outweighed him by 29 kg (64 (lb) and was a decorated freestyle wrestler, and their match would have no time limit. Helio was positive claiming he would submit Ebert in a short time; however, the bout lasted almost two hours and was eventually stopped by the police at the promoter's discretion as the fighting was not progressing or advancing position. It was later revealed that Gracie had to undergo an urgent operation the next day and the doctor demanded a stop due to Helio having a high fever caused by swelling. In 1955 Gracie was challenged by Valdemar Santana, a former student of his academy who now fought and trained under the management of Carlos Renato and Heraldo Brito. That challenge ended with Santana lifted Gracie up and slammed him on the mat and then landed a soccer kick to the head of a kneeling Gracie. Gracie was knocked out and his cornermen threw the towel. Gracie's bout with Santana was his final match before his retirement. His son Rorion was among the first family members to bring Gracie Jiu-Jitsu to the United States. The legacy of Gracie's anything goes in matches continues in the modern sport of mixed martial arts in which Brazilian jiu-jitsus become a key technique; the Gracie fighting system is now one of the most popular martial arts in the world. Helio Gracie died at age 95 in Brazil on 29 January 2009.

Mike Huckabee (402)

Mike Huckabee was born August 24, 1955 in Hope Arkansas; his ancestry is English, German, and Scottish-Irish, with roots in America dating back to the Colonial Era. He has cited his working-class upbringing as the reason for his political views. His father worked as a fireman and mechanic, and his mother was a clerk at a gas company. Mike landed his first job at age 14 where he was reading the news and the weather, at a radio station. At age 19 he married Janet McCain and 4 years later graduated from Ouachita Baptist University, completing his Bachelors degree in religion before attending Southwestern Baptist Theological Seminary in Fort Worth Texas. After one year there he dropped out to take a job in Christian Broadcasting, and at age 21 he was a staffer for televangelist James Robison. After working with James Robison, he said this about Mike Huckabee: "His convictions shape his character and his character will shape his policies; his whole life has been shaped by moral absolutes." Prior to his political career, he served as pastor at Immanuel Baptist Church in Pine Bluff Arkansas from 1980 to 1986, from 1986 to 1992 at First Baptist Church on Beech Street at Texarkana. He started 24-hour TV Stations at Pine Bluff and Texarkana where he produced documentaries and hosted a program called *Positive Alternatives*. He listened to countless young couples pour out their souls as they struggled to get their marriages into survival mode especially when confronted with overextended debt. In 1989 he was elected president of the Arkansas Baptist State Convention and served in that capacity to 1991. After that he was elected to Lt Governor but recalls a chilly reception finding the doors to the office nailed shut from the inside, office furniture was removed. After 59 days of public outcry the doors were finally opened. In 1994 he was re-elected with 59% of the vote and later became governor of Arkansas. He received widespread response of how he handled hurricane Katrina; in 2005 *Time* named him one of the five best governors in the US. In 2006 AARP awarded him with their impact award for his health initiatives. By the end of his term, he was the governor who had served (the third longest tenure of any Arkansas governor). Mike has won and lost some of his political endeavors, but has consistently credited God with all his successes. He has made attempts to run for the White House but was never able to attract enough support to make that a winning ticket. Mike Huckabee is the father of former White House Press Secretary Sarah Huckabee Sanders, and after he served as 44th Governor of Arkansas from 1996 to 2007, he had the privilege to launch the Governors race for his daughter Sarah who should not face too many obstacles in such endeavors.

Lawrence B. Jones (403)

Lawrence Billy Jones III was born on 10 December 1992 in Texas US. He was raised by his mother, Tameria and father Lawrence Jones II. He was chosen and served as "youth Mayor" of Garland Texas in 2009, and graduated from Garland high school in 2011. His activism apparently was in his bones and he became known before he graduated from High School. Thereafter he studied political science and criminal justice at the University of North Texas. He was hired as a student advocate in the Garland independent school district, becoming their youngest employee. He was a positive individual and at age 19 ran for a seat on the school board for his district, but lost the election, he was young and was not discouraged but was very understanding of what happens when you first try, he was realistic and knew when u have aspirations to serve in public office you quickly discover sometimes you win and other times you lose. He kept on pushing forward and served two years as a board member for Dallas County Child Welfare. In 2016 Jones was on the Garland Parks and Recreation Board. In 2013 he was named Activist of the Year by Freedom Works. That same year he was asked by Project Veritas, a conservative organization founded by James O'Keefe which is known for publishing secretly recorded videos exposing allegations of vendors who enrolled individuals in the healthcare marketplace mostly of the Patient Protection and Affordable Care Act. (This next item is one of the prime reasons he is in this book). He was a 21-year-old single young man and noticed in the media that a pizza shop called _Memories Pizza in Indiana_ had been forced to close after receiving backlash when its owners said they would refuse to cater a gay wedding if asked. To Jones it was not just a news item; he went to the owner and said: "I like to hold a fundraiser for you", did so and raised $844,000 for the family, which was used in part for bills and the rest donated to charity and the owner's church. Don't overlook the fact that he was only 21 years old at that time. In May 2018 he claimed on Fox News that because ESPN personality Jemele Hill was unemployed; she therefore did not deserve a journalism award from the National Association of Black Journalists and that the NABJ was seeking to "applaud unemployment". In April 2019, Jones did a Fox News Segment at the Mexico border in Laredo Texas. He was subsequently mocked on line, for wearing a bullet proof vest. In that same year Jones blamed the Barack Obama Administration for a lenient plea deal that sex offender and accused child sex trafficker Jeffrey Epstein received in 2008. He is a very young 28-year-old political commentator, radio host and author currently serving as a correspondent contributor for Fox News and already comes across as an experienced reporter; he will go far in life and belongs on these pages.

Steve Hilton (404)

Steve Hilton was born on 25 August 1969 in the United Kingdom. His original name was Hircsak; when Steve was about 13 years old, his parents were immigrants who came to Great Britain during the Hungarian revolution of 1956. His parents claimed asylum and anglicized their name to Hilton. Steve's father had been a goaltender for the Hungarian national ice hockey team and was considered one of the top ice hockey players in Europe in the 1930's. After arriving in Britain his parents initially worked in catering at Heathrow Airport, and divorced when Steve was five years old, leading to what he described as a struggle and great financial hardship; his mother worked in a shoe store but was primarily dependent on state benefits, and the two lived in a cold damp basement apartment. He studied at Christ's hospital school at Horsham, after that Steve studied philosophy, economics, and politics at New College at Oxford University; after graduating he worked at Conservative Central Office where he came to know Rachael Whetstone, who later became his wife. He was a strategist for Prime Minister David Cameron, and worked with him to re-brand the Conservative party as Green and Progressive. In 2015 he joined the UK think tank policy and exchange as a visiting scholar, then published his book *More Human* in May of that year; the book advocates smaller, human scale organizations and is critical of large governmental and businesses, including factory farms and banks. Then he spent a year as a visiting fellow at Stanford University's Hoover Institution and Freeman Spogli Institute for International Studies. In November 2016 while writing for Fox News he announced his support for Donald Trump over Hillary Clinton in the presidential election. In 2019 Hilton claimed that CNN, MSNBC, former CIA director John Brennan and former director of National Intelligence James Clapper as well as Democratic Congress member Adam Schiff and Eric Swalwell were the "real agents of Putin" for playing a role in "dividing" the United States over Trump's alleged ties with Russia. In 2020, during the COVID-19 pandemic in the United States, and shortly after social distancing measures and lockdowns were implemented, Hilton called on President Trump to end the measures; and criticized *"our ruling class and their TV mouthpieces"* for whipping up fear over this virus. He suggested that *"The cure could be worse than the disease."* In the year 2021, Steve became an American citizen and has never been shy before, and after, to speak his mind about the political issues that have been very much part of our lives in Great Britain as well as America. Steve Rachael were Godparents of David Cameron's son Ivan, who died at age six in Feb. 25, 2009. Since 2017 Steve Hilton has presented the weekly program: *The Next Revolution* on Fox News.

Dinesh D'Souza (405)

Dinesh Joseph D'Souza was born April 25, 1961 in Bombay (now Mumbai) India, his parents were Roman Catholics from the state of Goa in Western India, where his father was an executive with Johnson and Johnson and his mother was a housewife. He attended the Jesuit St. Stanislaus High School in Bombay, and completed his 11th and 12th year at Sydenham College, also in Bombay. In 1978 he became a foreign exchange student and traveled to the United States under the Rotary Youth Exchange and attended the local public school in Patagonia Arizona. From there he moved on to matriculate a Dartmouth College, from where he graduated with a Bachelor of Arts in English in 1983 and was a member of Phi Beta Kappa; while at Dartmouth D'Souza wrote for the Dartmouth Review an independent student edited alumni a Collegiate Network subsidized publication. There he faced much criticism during his time at the Review for authoring an article publicly outing homosexual members of the school's Gay Straight Alliance student organization. After graduating from Dartmouth, D'Souza became the editor of a monthly journal called *The Prospect*, a publication financed by a group of Princeton University Alumni. The paper and the writers ignited much controversy during D'Souza's editorship by, among other things, criticizing the college's affirmative action policies. After College he became a political commentator and provocateur and certainly had a neck for attracting controversy, it seemed like whenever he opened his mind he was immersed in controversy. In 1995 he published *The End of Racism* in which he claimed that exaggerated claims of racism are holding back progress among African Americans, whether he was right or wrong, is not the issue, D'Souza was not afraid to say it, and then defend it. It is that what makes him a popular speaker, for example: he claimed that exaggerated claims of racism are holding back progress among African Americans in the US. He said: "The American slave was treated like property, which is to say, pretty well". If his goal was controversy, he certainly got that, at minimum, it sells books. Someone wrote in "*The Journal of Southern History*" His book is flawed, he ignores the complex causes and severity of white racism, misrepresents people's arguments, and undervalues the matrix of ignorance, fear, and long-term economic inequality that he dubs black cultural pathology. Another wrote: D'Souza's trivialized racism and said: "much of what Souza said is untrue, or only partially true, where selected facts are pulled out of any recognizable context and used to support a particular viewpoint." Whether that is true or not, I likely could fill this book with 200 liberals who qualify of such assertions; I happen to be a fan of Dinesh D'Souza's essays, books, films and documentaries, and do believe he makes a difference.

David Hume (406)

David Hume was born May 7, 1711 in Edinburgh Scotland, United Kingdom, and is generally regarded as one of the most important philosophers to write in English, and as far as I can tell he was well known in his time as an historian, essayist, and a master stylist in any genre; (there may be a lot more, but these are <u>some</u> of his major philosophical works: <u>A treatise of human nature</u> (1739, 1740), <u>The enquiries concerning human understanding</u> (1748), and <u>Concerning the Principals of Morals</u> (1751), and his posthumously published <u>Dialogues concerning Natural Religion</u> (1779); still today his writings remain widely and deeply influential. Having said that and not being an expert in that discipline, I feel compelled to comment here that Hume's more conservative contemporaries denounced his writings as works of skepticism, and atheism, but his influence is evident in the moral philosophy and economic writings of his close friend Adam Smith, likely best described by Dennis C. Rasmussen in <u>The Infidel and the Professor</u>: arguably the greatest friendship in the history of philosophy. Kant reported that Hume's work "<u>woke him from his dogmatic slumbers</u>"; Jeremy Bentham remarked that Hume "<u>caused the scales to fall from his eyes</u>. Charles Darwin regarded his work as a central influence, on the theory of evolution. If what you see here may makes you puzzled, as it did me, <u>or</u>, perhaps more succinctly stated: leave you confused to find such diverse opinions which these writers took from what they gleaned from reading his observation; and then reflect both the richness of their sources and the wide range of his empiricism; (perhaps more of a 17th century word but can not find another expression for it; I was not trained in the fundamental principles of this language.) On <u>causality</u> he writes for example one action follows another; if rain falls to the ground, the grass gets wet. Why is the grass wet? Because rain came down from the sky! How would you like to sit in a class where such items are endlessly debated? Here is Bertrand Russell's opinion: If everything must have a cause, then God must have a cause. You see why I do not want to get us in to a philosophical debate. One of my very close friends holds an Eastern and Western PhD in philosophy; we remain close friends if we leave those topics in the closet. Here are some of Hume's expressions he has left for us to chew on: "<u>The role of reason is not to make us wise but to reveal our ignorance</u>" … "<u>I do not have enough faith to believe there is no God</u>" … "<u>A little Philosophy makes a man an atheist, a great deal converts him to religion</u>" … <u>It is not reason which is the guide of life, but custom</u>". David Hume died in Edinburgh Scotland on August 25, 1776; he left a legacy of influence on such people as Immanuel Kant, Adam Smith, John Stuart Mill and many more.

Keli'i Akina (407)

Keli'i was blest with an amazing mother who insisted that before he was allowed to run off and play, he had reading assignments, not "*yes mom I read the book*", no! His mother Marian insisted: read it loud to me, this began at an age when little boys climb on mommy's lap to read. She told him: Read louder, pronounce better, she made sure that her children received a proper education and learn. One of her proudest moments came when her son became a champion debater and orator at Kamehameha Schools, that ability has served Keli'i well throughout his life. After graduating from Kamehameha schools he went to Northwestern University, there he was impacted by a Campus Speaker called Billy Graham, and after that moved to Hawaii to serve high school youth on the Wai'anai coast where for three decades he operated crisis-intervention programs for Youth for Christ and served as a key person in the program called Center for Tomorrow's Leaders; it is in these programs that I got to know him rather well; in those years I served as chairman of the YFC board for about 30 years, and also served with Dick Rowland on an organization called Grassroots. In the meantime, Keli'i connected with Beijing University, and never stopped his pursuit of learning and holds a Ph-D degree in East and Western philosophy. He was founder of the Center for Tomorrows Leaders he has from time to time credited me with his political interest, although I believe that is an overstatement; He has successfully acquired an elected political seat as a trustee on the Office of Hawaiian Affairs (OHA) and consistently pulls other OHA board members back to focus on the real bread and butter issues that benefit Hawaiian people, such as Housing, Jobs, Education and Health Care. Countless Hawaiians are struggling just to make ends meet, therefore Keli'i is lazar focused on these issues, and refused to accept the "*hand out*" of $44,400 given to OHA beneficiaries. Homesteaders must aggressively pursue commercial development that generates revenue like the Bishop Estate has done through shopping centers and other commercial ventures, like they have done with schools. What about the 30-meter telescope on top of Mauna Kea? There is room for both science and the sacred, this is in keeping with the centuries old values of Hawaiians who navigated by the stars; we must unite not divide. Many Hawaiians are proud to be Hawaiians and American; OHA should foster economic empowerment for all Hawaiians. When Hawaiians suffer everyone suffers, when Hawaiians prosper, everyone prospers; Midweek newspaper features Keli'i Akina on its cover 29 September 2021.

Victor Davis Hanson (408)

Victor Davis Hanson was born September 5, 1953 in Fowler California. His family is of Protestant Swedish and Welsh descent, he grew up in California on the family raisin farm outside Selma in the San Joaquin Valley and has worked there most of his life. His mother Pauline was a lawyer and a California superior court and state appeals court justice, his father was a farmer, educator, and junior college administrator. Victor attended public schools and graduated from Selma High School, received his B.A. with highest honors in classics and general college honors at Cowell College, from the University of California Santa Cruz, in 1975; he earned his Ph.D. in the classics from Stanford University in 1980. He won the Raphael Demos scholarship at the college year in Athens 1973-74) and was a regular member of the American School of Classical Studies Athens (1078-79). He is a Senior Fellow at the Hoover Institution and professor emeritus at California State University where he began teaching in 1984; there he created the classical studies program. Since 2004 Hanson has written a weekly column syndicated by Tribune Content Agency, as well as a weekly column by National Review Online since 2001 and has not missed a weekly column for either venue since he began. He has been published in the New York Times, Wall Street Journal, The Daily Telegraph, American Heritage, and other publications. He co-authored the book *Who Killed Homer*? The *Demise of Classical Education*, and *Recovery of Greek Wisdom*, with John Heath. The book explores the issue of how classical education has declined in the US and what might be done to restore it to its former prominence. This is important according to Hanson and Heath because knowledge of the classical Greeks and Romans is necessary to understand Western culture. Hanson has supported Donald Trump from the beginning, authoring a 2019 book: *The case for Trump*. He wrote about race relations in response to Eric Holder's *talk to his son*, this prompted Hanson to write a column *Facing Facts about Race*; in there he offered his own version of *the talk*, namely the need to inform children to be careful of young black men when venturing in to the inner city, who Hanson argues are statistically more likely to commit violent crime than young men of other races and that therefore it is understandable for the police to focus on them. Another writer described Hanson's column as stupid advice. Is racial sensitivity stupid? What if he said: I like Asian Americans to do my taxes because they are better on math: *or*, I would like my son to marry a Jewish girl because Jews are successful people, would that be stupidity, or just be prudent, or neither? Hanson is an award-winning scholar and a man with inborn wisdom has written more than 25 books, and is often asked for advice on complex issues.

Robert Vernon (409)

Robert Vernon rose to the level of assistant police chief of the 8400 police force in the city of Los Angeles; a formidable accomplishment that most police never reach regardless how good they may be, the media refer to Bob like this: "...<u>the word in the department and in City Hall was that the best way to win promotions and good assignments was to accept Vernon's religious views</u>; another said: "<u>...he's head of the God Squad as we refer to it...it is commonly known that the way you get ahead as far as Vernon is concerned, is to become aligned with his church, or to profess that you are born again</u>." (In case you wonder what was Bob's Church? It is Grace Community church, which was founded in 1956 and is currently one of the larger Evangelical churches in the Los Angeles area, now pastured by John MacArthur, (former Police chaplain at the Los Angeles Police Department), and has become <u>"the church that never sleeps."</u> due to its ministry outreach across the entire world." We have worshipped there and were invited to a dinner with Pastor Mac Arthur.) Back to Vernon, he has tasted much of the media's venom. Why? Because he's Evangelical Christian and speaks to young people on this topic: Can a cop who meets crime and violence everyday really be a peacemaker? Can a man of faith perform the duties of his job he swore to and still honor the God he firmly believes in? Bob Vernon's 38-year career as a cop, a former assistant chief of police for Los Angeles, the son of a cop and grandfather of 4 cops answers these with a resounding <u>YES</u>. After years of experience, Bob Vernon became the commander and rose to the role of assistant deputy chief. (I have a brother, although in another country, who also served as a police chief, and may perhaps show my bias a little). There may have been a time that America had an independent press but that may have been during the Civil War; Today if a person of notoriety wants to give credit to the God of heaven, "*the independent Press*" will label such person, and openly ridicule him and tauntingly respect such person as a joke; which is the treatment Bob received from the media, who preferred to call him <u>Bible Bob</u>, or <u>Reverend Bob</u>; had Bob been a Moslem, a Hindu, or simply been a member of any far left mainline Christian denomination, the media would not care. But Bob practiced what he believes while being an active member of Grace Community Church; we have a mutual friend there, a family who has lost a son in the ocean here, when they come to Hawaii, they always stop in our home; one time they brought Bob Vernon and it is in that setting we had the privilege of meeting him at our home. In 2018 we received an e-mail from Hume Lake (Bob served as a member of the Board of Directors) and asked for healing and recovery for chief Vernon.

Eric Metaxas (410)

Eric Metaxas was born 27 June, 1963 in Queens New York he is Greek on his father's side and grew up in Danbury Connecticut. Eric graduated from Yale University (1984, B.A.), while there he edited the *Yale Record*. He is an American Christian author, speaker and conservative radio host; and has written three biographies, Amazing Grace: William Wilberforce (2007), Bonhoeffer: Pastor Martyr, Prophet, Spy, (2011) and Martin Luther, (2017) the man who rediscovered God and changed the world. Eric has a radio program *The Eric Metaxas Show*. He was raised in the Greek Orthodox environment, while he has not formally left it; he attends Central Presbyterian Church, and describes himself as a "Mere Christian;" after the words of C.S. Lewis. In 2007 while talking about his books he said: My books don't touch upon anything at all where Protestants, Catholics, and Orthodox Christians differ. They only talk about the Christian faith that they have agreement on. May be so but that did not keep Eric out of controversy; in his book Martin Luther he criticized the power structures that had emerged from the medieval Catholic Church, that it was only with Luther, that the true Gospel was rescued "from under its crushing welter of ecclesiastical and political medieval structures". He has not escaped the criticism of the right and the left when he began writing about these historical giants, and I am sure he was expecting that; Metaxas has been a prominent supporter of Donald Trump and has not been quiet about the fact that this election was tainted with voter fraud; he was not a lone voice in that opinion. He has published two children's books called *Donald builds the wall* and *Donald drains the swamp* in a series called Donald the Caveman. Characters in the book he called an angry little girl who looks a little like AOC, and an angry crazy old man who looks a lot like Bernie. In the late 1990's Metaxas wrote Break-Point radio commentaries for Prison Fellowship Founder Chuck Colson. Upon Colson's death in 2012 Metaxas along with John Stonestreet, became the voice of which now airs weekdays on 1350 outlets across the country. On February 2, 2012 Metaxas was the keynote speaker at the National Prayer Breakfast. He has testified before Congress about the rise of anti-Semitism in the U.S. and abroad. He was awarded the Becket Fund's Canterbury Medal in 2011 and the Human Life Review's Defender of Life Award in 2013. Metaxas has received honorary doctorate degrees from Hillsdale College, Liberty University, Sewanee, The University of the South Ohio Christian University, and Colorado Christian University, some of his writings have been published in the Atlantic Monthly, New York Times and the Wall Street Journal. In 2021 amid the COVID-19 pandemic, Metaxas told his followers "Don't get the vaccine."

Irving Copi (411)

Irving Copi was born July 28, 1917 Copilowish, in Duluth, Minnesota, there he was captain of the debate team at South Central High and later was Chess champion of Ann Arbor in 1935. He was inspired by, and studied under, Bertrand Russell at the Univ. of Chicago, who in 1948 cited Copi in his autobiography as one of his 3 best and brightest students. Copi contributed to the calculus of relations with his article using logical matrices, and received numerous academic honors, including Guggenheim and Ford Foundation fellowships, and a Fulbright-Hays Senior Research Fellowship. He did seminal work in the development of computers, co-authoring the logical design of an idealized General-Purpose Computer in 1954, authoring artificial languages in 1958 and Realization of Events by Logical Nets with Elgot and Wright in 1958. He taught at the University of Illinois, the United States Air Force Academy, Princeton, and the Georgetown University Logic Institute, the University of Michigan (1958-1969). After that purchased a home near my office in Waialae Iki and taught at the University of Hawaii from 1969 to 1990. He was married to Amelia Glaser; they had 4 children David, Thomas, William and Margaret. While teaching Logic, Copi was assigned to review textbooks and decided to write his own. The manuscript was split into Introduction to Logic and Symbolic Logic. A reviewer noted that it had an unusually comprehensive chapter in definition and the author accounts for the seductive nature of informal fallacies. The textbooks proved popular, and a reviewer of the third edition noted over 100 new exercises added. Both textbooks are widely used, with the former currently in its 14th edition. My friend studied under him and got his Ph. D degree under him told me that Irving Copi was one of the most recognized scholars in the field of Philosophy in the entire world. He was the type of person, if you were his friend; you remained so no matter what professional differences might arise. I had a financial office with about 8000 clients and about 100 of those were University faculty. He was Jewish and discovered that I had grown up under Hitler in World War II and many families in our area had helped rescue Jewish Children from Amsterdam. He was greatly interested in that era of what happened to the Jewish population in Europe. He knew I was a child but wanted to know what it was like growing up during the days of Anne Frank and Corrie Ten Boom. He brought his coffee or whatever he had in that cup and loved to sit down and talk story, although he was my senior by almost 20 years, as well as being a brilliant scholar and I was not in the world of academia, just a simple business man, but chatting with him was like we had been brothers for a lifetime. Irving Copi died peacefully at home in Honolulu at age 85 on August 19, 2002; I miss him.

Cesar Pelli (412)

Cesar Pelli was born October 12, 1926 in Argentina; his father was a civil servant who struggled through the Depression, while his mother worked as a teacher. Pelli studied architecture at the Universidad Nacional de Tucuman, and graduated in 1949, after which he designed low-cost housing projects. He married acclaimed landscape architect Diana Balmori, who became his partner in more ways than one. In 1952 Pelli and his wife moved to the United States and became naturalized citizens in 1964, they had 2 children; Denis, a Neurobiologist and Professor of Psychology, and Rafael, became a well-known architect. In 1952 he attended the University of Illinois school of architecture for advanced study in architecture and got his Master of Science is Architecture degree in 1954. They resided in The San Remo on Manhattan's Upper West Side. One of his early projects was the TWA Terminal at John F. Kennedy Airport. In 1968 Pelli became partner for design at Gruen Associates in Los Angeles, in 1969, Pelli designed the COMSAT research and development laboratories in Clarksburg, Maryland, and designed his first landmark building with the Pacific Design Center in West Hollywood, California, which was completed 1975 and became known by the locals as the Blue Whale; the United States Embassy in Tokyo, Japan was designed by Pelli in 1972 and completed in 1975; while practicing in Los Angeles Pelli taught in the architecture program at UCLA. In 1977, Pelli was selected to be the dean of the Yale School of Architecture in New Haven Connecticut and served in that post until 1984. Shortly after his arrival at Yale he won the commission to design the expansion and renovation of the Museum of Modern Art in New York which resulted in the establishment of his own firm Cesar Pelli and Associates. The Museum's expansion/renovation and the Museum of Modern Art Residential Tower were completed in 1984; The World Financial Center in New York, which includes the grand public space of the Winter Garden, was completed in 1988. Among other significant projects he has designed are: the Crile Clinic building in Cleveland Ohio, completed 1984, The Plaza Tower in Costa Mesa California (1991) The National Museum of Art in Osaka Japan (2005), The Adrienne Arsht Center for Performing Arts in Miami Florida, in 1991 Pelli was named one of the ten most influential living American Architects by the American Institute of Architects. In 1995 he was awarded the American Institute of Architects Gold Medal. Cesar Pelli was the creator of incredible buildings such as Kuala Lumpur's Petronas Towers, New York's MoMa's renovation; his work has left a mark on architecture world wide. On July 19, 2019 at age 92 the world lost one of the greatest architects and designers when Cesar Pelli died at his home in New Haven Connecticut.

Augustine of Hippo (413)

Aurilius Augustinus Hipponensis was born 13 November 354 in Thagaste, Numidia Cirtensis, Western Roman Empire now Algeria. As far as I can determine it is the region we call today North Africa near Tunisia, Libya, Mauritania, Niger, Morocco or somewhere south of the Mediterranian Sea. We shall refer to him as Augustine, or Saint Augustine. His mother Monica was a devout Christian, his father Patricius was a pagan who converted on his deathbed to Christianity. In his writings he leaves some information about his African heritage, for example he referred to someone as the most notorious <u>of us Africans</u>. His first insight into the nature of sin came when he and a number of friends stole fruit from a neighborhood garden. He tells that story in his autobiography <u>*The Confessions*</u>, he remembers he did not steal the fruit because he was hungry, but because it was not permitted; his very nature he says was flawed and concluded the human person is naturally inclined to sin and in need of the grace of Christ. At age 11 he was sent to school about 19 miles south. There he became familiar with Latin literature as well as pagan beliefs and practices. At age 17 he had a relationship with a young woman, but his mother wanted him to marry someone of his class and warned him to avoid sex outside of marriage, he kept the relationship for 15 years and she gave birth to his son, <u>Adeodatus</u> (meaning; Gift from God). His writings and his thoughts profoundly influenced the development of Western philosophy, and Western Christianity; He is viewed as one of the most important Church Fathers of the Latin Church in the <u>Patristic Period</u>, (*the period from the Apostle John to perhaps somewhere around 450 AD*); some of his important works are <u>*The City of God*</u>, (in there he imagined the church as a spiritual City of God, distinct from the material Earthly City). His thoughts profoundly influenced the medieval worldview; the segment of the church that adhered to the concept of the Trinity as defined by the Council of Nicaea (325), and the Council of Constantinople (381), closely identified with Augustine on the Trinity. Other important works of his are: <u>*On Christian Doctrine*</u>, and <u>*Confessions*</u>. According to his contemporary, Jerome, Augustine established anew the ancient Faith. After his conversion to Christianity and baptism in 386 Augustine developed his own approach to philosophy and theology accommodating a variety of methods and perspectives. The Catholic Church, the Eastern Orthodox Church, and the Anglican Communion, recognize Augustine as a saint. Many Protestants, especially Calvinists and Lutherans consider him one of the fathers of the Protestant Reformation, due to his teachings on salvation and divine grace. Augustine died at age 75 on August 28, in the year 430.

William H Parker (414)

William Henry Parker III was born 21 June 1905 in Lead South Dakota U.S. and was raised in Deadwood. His grandfather was an American Civil War veteran who later served in congress. The family migrated to Los Angeles California in 1922 for better opportunities, at a time when California was the place to be in America. He originally wanted to be an attorney, and studied at several colleges, after that he joined the Los Angeles Police Department in 1927 and continued his legal studies, he graduated with an LL.B degree in 1930 and passed the bar exam, but opted to continue with the police department instead of practicing law. He was an active advocate for the police and fire fighter's union thereby creating job security and better wages. He served as an officer on the force for 15 years before taking a leave to fight in World War II in Sardinia, Normandy, Munich, and Frankfurt and for his injuries received a Purple Heart. After the war he returned to LAPD and rose to the rank of captain and rapidly ascended through the ranks and was soon appointed Chief of Police on August 9, 1950, he served in that position till he died in 1966. During his tenure he has been credited with bringing the LAPD to the forefront as a world renowned law enforcement agency. He was credited with many changes in the police academy some were similar to military peacekeeping methods to which he was exposed during the war. Although he had a low opinion of Hollywood and how it portrayed American Law Enforcement, he did conclude that it could become an effective tool that might be helpful to law enforcement; he even helped with the production of *The Thin Blue Line*. Much more influential was his support for radio and TV program *Dragnet*. He often gave Jack Webb access to police files and allowed them to observe LAPD in action. Accuracy was a major goal of *Dragnet*, Webb (with Parker's approval), was a strong advocate of LAPD and as a courtesy stayed away from stories that showed any measure of incompetence or corruption. He did appear on the popular TV program: *What's my line* one time as a guest. While serving as chief he reduced police corruption and cleaned up the overall image of the police, although the vice squad and reserve force continued to remain controversial elements such as the Organized Crime and Intelligence Division of the LAPD to keep tabs on suspected politicians and their mafia syndicate allies as well as the notoriously corrupt and narcotic-ridden Hollywood movie industry and its celebrities. He faced and dealt with police brutalities, and racism toward the African American and Latino residents. He is credited with being the longest serving chief in the LAPD history, serving in that position from 1950 to 1966. He died at age 61 on 16 July 1966 in Los Angeles. The former headquarters of LAPD was re-named in his honor.

Millard Dean Fuller (415)

Millard Dean Fuller was born January 3, 1935 in Lanett Alabama U.S. His mother died in 1938 at age 27, leaving behind a young man with a 3-year-old child, and his father remarried in 1941 to Eunice Stephens. The family was self employed with a small grocery store, ice cream shop, and a small farm. Millard Dean got an economics degree in 1957, received a law degree from the University of Alabama. He married Linda Caldwell of Tuscaloosa, and became a successful businessman, and self-made millionaire by age 29. In 1968 after giving up their wealth they re-focused their lives on Christian service, Dean and Linda moved with their children to an interracial community in southwest Georgia to Koinonia Farm, founded by Clarence Jordan in 1942, it became home to the Fuller family for 5 years until they moved as missionaries with the Christian Church to Zaire, (*now the Democratic Republic of the Congo*). There began work in Mbandaka, a city of extreme poverty; they oversaw and began work that would be a first step in the international housing industry; undeveloped land in the center of Mbandaka was given by the government for the purpose of building a 100 free standing units house development. In 1976 the Fullers returned to the United States and began a Christian ministry Koinonia Farm building simple decent homes for low-income families in their community using volunteer labor and donations, requiring repayment only for the cost of the materials used. No interest charged as is done with regular mortgages and no profit was made; it was called Partnership Housing which grew into a larger scale ministry known as *Habitat for Humanity International*; Concerned residents worked with the Fullers, that idea took hold in Appalachia and by 1981; (just 5 years from its inception), *Habitat for Humanity International* had affiliates in 14 states and 7 foreign countries. Later in 2005 a dispute between the Fullers and the board of directors, came to a head over allegedly sexual misconduct by Fuller. In March 2005 amid allegations of inappropriate behavior by him toward a female employee the Fullers were forced to resign their leadership post. Fuller continued his work in the housing movement, and expanded on the foundation of Habitat by encouraging communities to create collaborate partnerships to address the housing needs. Fuller received numerous awards and more than 50 honorary degrees. He devoted his life to address the housing needs for those who are too poor to buy one. Millard Dean Fuller died unexpectedly at age 74 on February 3, 2009 while en route to the hospital in Albany Georgia; his remains are buried on the grounds of Koinonia Farm, Habitat for Humanity builds a 3-bedroom 1200 Sq ft home, and has helped 35 million people in all 50 states and more than 70 foreign countries.

Julia Child (416)

Julia Carolyn Mc Williams Child was born August 15, 1912 in Pasadena California, and attended Polytechnic School from the 4th grade to the 9th Grade in Pasadena, then went to Katherine Branson School in Ross, California, at 6 ft 2 inches she played tennis, golf and basketball; after high school she attended Smith College Massachusetts, from which she graduated in 1934 with a major in history. She grew up in a family with a cook, but did not learn cooking from this person, and never learned until she met Paul who grew up in a family who loved food. After college she moved to New York and worked as a copywriter for an advertising co. Then came World War II and in 1942 she joined the office of Strategic Services (OSS), and discovered she was too tall to enlist in the Women'sArmy Corps (WAC) or in the US Navy's WAVES and began her OSS career as a typist at its headquarters in Washington and with her education and experience, was soon given a more responsible position as a top-secret researcher working directly for General William J. Donovan, there was an assistant in the Secret Intelligence Division, and typed 10,000 names on white note cards. For a year, she worked at the OSS emergency Sea Rescue Equipment Section (ERES) first as file clerk; later as an assistant to developers of a shark repellent needed to ensure that sharks would not explode ordnance targeting German U-boats. From 1944-1945 she was posted to Ceylon where her responsibilities included registering, a great volume of highly classified communications. When she was asked to solve the curious shark problem, her solution was experiment with cooking various concoctions as a shark repellent, marked Child's first foray in to the world of cooking. For her service she was cited and awarded for here many virtues and her drive and inherent cheerfulness. Then she became the lady who was the French Chef who was neither French nor Chef. But became the star of numerous TV programs and had a major impact on American households teaching America how to cook, whether it was French Cuisine, Indian Curry, Mexican tortillas topped with salsa, or just a simple TV Dinner, Julia Child had the answers. Then she added the American Institute of wine and food. She also became concerned about Children's food education. She starred in four more series that featured guest chefs and collaborated with Jacques Pepin many times for television programs and cookbooks for home cooking. Her use of butter and cream was often questioned by food critics. Her husband designed the kitchen with high counters for her height. She died on August 13, 2004 just two days before her 92nd birthday. In 1995 she arranged to establish the Julia Child Foundation which was later moved to California to protect her legacy.

William Worrall Mayo (417)

William Worrall Mayo was born May 31, 1819 in Salford Lancashire England and studied science in Manchester under John Dalton the chemist and physicist responsible for formulating the modern atomic theory of matter and devising a table of relative atomic weights. He was a descendant of a famous English Chemist, John Mayao; in 1846 he migrated to the United States, where his first work in the new world was a pharmacist at Belleview hospital in New York city, though he did not stay there and soon moved westward; after sometime in Buffalo New York he settled in Lafayette, Indiana where he worked as a tailor (one of the vocations he had while in England). He returned to medicine in 1849 assisting in a cholera outbreak working at Indiana medical college; the training there would probably be considered mediocre by modern standards, the school did have a microscope an uncommon tool at that time. His graduation was orally reported in 1850 however no documentation exists of that. He then attended and graduated from the University of Missouri with a degree in medicine in 1854; and tried his hand at different activities, even farming, and operating a ferry service, serving as justice of the peace and did occasional medical duties. Two more daughters were born after the flood. In 1859 the family moved to a home on Main Street in Sueur, and set up a medical practice but having not enough patients he tried publishing a newspaper which lasted only 3 months. At the beginning of the Civil War in 1861 he tried a commission as military surgeon but was rejected. He then attended the hanging of 38 Native Americans in December 1862 and was given a body he dissected in front of medical colleagues. In 1863 he was named examining surgeon for the 1st Minnesota draft board in Rochester, a year later son Charles Horace was born. In 1863 he opened a practice in Rochester with W. A. Hyde, but in 1864 went solo, in 1867 he attempted politics making a speech to expose local corruption which ended poorly. In 1880 Dr Mayo was elected city mayor he advocated unsuccessfully to create an artificial lake. That event is often credited with beginning the "*Mayo Clinic Story*" when on August 21, 1883 a tornado devastated Rochester, many patients needed intensive care beyond what was being provided by relatives and friends. It was later in 1910 he became interested in the extraction and distillation of alcohol from animal waste and one day suffered a serious accident when the mechanism crushed his arm which necessitated amputation, serious complication resulted in his death in March 1911 shortly before his 92nd birthday his wife died in 1915, they are buried next to each other in Rochester. It was his medical practice which later evolved by his sons that became the world-renowned Mayo Clinic.

John Dalton (418)

John Dalton was born 6 September 1766 in Eaglesfield Cumberland, England into a Quaker family. His father was a weaver, and John received his early education from him, and from Quaker John Fletcher, who ran a private school in a nearby village. Dalton never married and had very few friends, as a Quaker he lived a modest and unassuming personal life. He lived in a room in the home of the Rev. W. Johns, a published botanist and his wife in George Street Manchester, (actually Dalton and Johns died in the same year in 1844). Dalton's daily round of laboratory work and tutoring was broken only by annual excursions to the Lake District and occasional visits to London. In 1822 he made a short trip to Paris where he met many distinguished resident men in science. Dalton was an English chemist, physicist and meteorologist, and is best known for introducing the atomic theory into chemistry, as well as for his research in to color blindness, sometimes referred to as Daltonism in his honor. The main points of Dalton's atomic theory as it eventually developed are: **1**: Elements are made of extremely small particles called atoms, **2**: Atoms of a given element are identical in size, mass and other properties; atoms of different elements differ in size, **3**: Atoms can not be subdivided, created, or destroyed. **4**: Atoms of different elements combine in simple whole-number ratios to form chemical compounds, **5**: In chemical reactions, atoms are combined, separated or rearranged. Even before he had propounded the atomic theory, Dalton had attained a considerable scientific reputation; in 1893, he was chosen to give a series of lectures on natural philosophy at the Royal Institution in London, and he delivered another series in 1809 -1810; some critics reported that he was deficient in the qualities that make an attractive lecturer, being harsh and indistinct in voice. (Not having met him in person, such comments come to me in this way: a brilliant scientist but not a charismatic communicator; I may be wrong, but that's what I pick up from these comments.) In 1810, Sir Humphrey Davy asked him to offer himself as a candidate for the fellowship of the Royal Society, but Dalton declined. In 1837 Dalton suffered a minor stroke and a second in 1838 leaving him with speech impairment, although he remained able to perform experiments; In May 1844 he had another stroke, and recorded with trembling hand his last meteorological observation. On 27 July, in Manchester, Dalton fell from his bed and was found lifeless by his attendant. He was accorded a civic funeral with full honors; his body lay in state in Manchester Town Hall for four days. More than 40,000 people filed past his coffin. The funeral procession included representatives of the cities major commercial and scientific communities.

Brandon Judd (419)

Brandon Judd is the President of Boarder Patrol guard, is widely known and highly regarded expert on border security and illegal immigration. He has served as a border patrol agent for the last 22 years and has been president of the National Border Patrol Council since March 2013. His dual roles include protecting America's borders while ensuring that the best interests of all rank-and-file Border Patrol Agents across the country are met. Mr. Judd is an extremely effective communicator; his border security positions have been covered by all forms of media; he has been called upon to testify before the US Congress as an expert witness on border security on numerous occasions, and is often consulted privately by policy makers on Capitol Hill. At the invitation of President Trump, Mr. Judd has participated with the President in multiple roundtables and Press Conferences both Pre-and Post election to discuss measures to effectively secure the border. Mr. Judd has written numerous border security op-eds that have been published by multiple media outlets including, but not limited to; USA Today, the Hill, Real Clear Politics, the Washington Times, and the Fox News National.

Due to Mr. Judd's advocacy numerous border security policies have been created and law enforcement operations implemented to ensure the safety and security of the United States and its citizens; Judd has testified at the following House Of Representatives before numerous Committees, and various topics such as: Oversight and Government Reform, Central American Immigrants and Border Security, Homeland Security, Subcommittee on Border and Maritime Security, Natural Resources, Subcommittee on oversight and Investigations, Hearing on Challenges Faced by Border Patrol Agents, Border Patrol from an Agent and officer perspective, The Border Wall Strengthening our National Security, Perspectives from the DHS Front line, Evaluating staffing Resources and Requirements, National security threats at our borders, the lawless immigration policies of the Obama Administration, America's Heroin Epidemic at the Border, Violence at the Border, an administration made disaster, Examining the surge of unaccompanied alien minors. It is no secret that the Democrats _want_ wide open borders; they never felt that way with us Europeans coming here in the 1950's and 60's. I have watched many of these hearings in the US House sub committees and it is very clear; Democrats want the borders wide open, for the same reason they oppose voter ID. _Knowing that,_ all these hearings are nothing more than an exercise in euphemism; Brandon Judd and his colleagues are to be commended to do what they do to keep America safe under extreme conditions, he should be awarded the Presidential Medal of Freedom.

Sabina Oster Wurmbrand (420)

Sabina Oster Wurmbrand was born July 10, 1913 in Czernowitz in the Austro-Hungarian Empire, which became Romania after WW-1 and part of Ukraine after WW-II. She was born in a Jewish family, and the town where she grew up was an important educational and cultural hub for the Jewish faith. She graduated from high school in Czernowitz and then studied languages at the Sorbonne in Paris. In 1936 at age 23 Sabina met and married Richard Wurmbrand, and while they were vacationing in the mountains of Romania, they were both converted to the Christian Faith and joined the Anglican Mission Church in Bucharest. Sabina's parents, 2 sisters and one brother were all killed in Nazi concentration camps and in the ensuing years the couple spent their time rescuing Jewish children from ghettos that they were forced to live in by the Nazi regime. They were arrested several times. After the war a million Russian troops poured in to Romania enabling the Communists to seize power, who attempted to control the churches, Richard and Sabina immediately began an underground ministry to their enslaved people, they traveled to Budapest smuggling goods and food to refugees. In 1946 to 1947 she organized and conducted religious meetings sometimes with gatherings up to 5,000 people. So effective was their work that Richard was arrested in 1948 and spent 14 years in Communist prisons, three of those years in solitary confinement, suffering much at the hands of his captors. There are few women in the world that had their faith tested like Sabina, though she never gave up her faith. During Richard's imprisonment Sabina continued to help the persecuted Church while struggling herself for survival for her and her young son. Eventually Sabina was arrested and spent three years in slave labor camps and prisons while her young son was forced to live on the streets. After being released she spent several years under house arrest. The communist leaders offered him freedom if she would divorce her husband and renounce her faith; she absolutely refused, then they told her that Richard had died in prison, but she did not believe any of that but clung to the hope that she would see her husband soon again. Richard was released from prison and returned home. They were ransomed for $10,000 and Richard was warned not to preach. They traveled to Scandinavia, England and to the United States where they testified before the Senate in Washington. In their freedom they organized a non-profit: "Voice of the Martyrs" to minister to those persecuted and imprisoned in Vietnam, China, North Korea, Cuba, Laos, and the former Soviet Union. She spoke to conferences, churches and prisons for 32 more years. Sabin Oster Wurmbrand died at age 87 on August 11, 2000 in California and Richard died one year later on February 17, 2001. They were married 63 years.

Mark A. Morgan (421)

Mark A Morgan was born January 1, 1950, and received a Juris Doctor degree from the University of Missouri-Kansas City School of Law, serving as a deputy sheriff with the Platte County Sheriff's Department in Missouri. He joined the United States Marine Corps at age 19 and served active duty and reserve for a total of 10 years concurrently with his studies; He had long career in the FBI culminating in appointments as head of the inspection Division and Training Division. As an American law enforcement official, he served as chief operating officer and acting commissioner of US Customs and border protection from July 2019 to January 2021. After law school he attended the Los Angeles Police Department Academy and after that served as a police officer with the LAPD field office; while there he was a member of the Eurasian Organized Crime Task Force, the Crime Task Force, the Crisis Response Squad and the Special Weapons and Tactics Team. In 2002 Morgan became a supervisory Special Agent and served as Crisis Management Coordinator in the Crisis Management Unit in the Critical Incident Response Group. In 2005, Morgan returned to Los Angeles where he supervised an FBI-led Hispanic Gang Task Force and focused on the MS-13, and 18th Street gangs. While in Los Angeles, he also supervised the Critical Incident Response Squad, which had administrative and operational oversight of the division's critical incident response resources. In 2007, Morgan became assistant section chief of the National Center for the analysis of Violent Crime Branch where he managed the FBI's behavioral Analyses Units and the Violent Crime Apprehension Program. In 2008 he became the FBI's Deputy on-Scene Commander in Baghdad Iraq where he was responsible for all FBI personnel deployed to Iraq under the auspices of the Counterterrorism Division. This was his first deployment to a war zone. In 2009 Morgan was assigned as Assistant Special Agent in charge of the New Haven Field Office. In 2010 he became Chief of the FBI Strategic Information and Operations Center. From 2011 to 2013 Morgan served as Special Agent in charge of the FBI El Paso Division. During 2013 and 2014 he served on a detail to US Customs and Border Protection (CBP) in the Department of Homeland Security as the Acting Assistant Commissioner for Internal Affairs. In this role he oversaw the investigation of criminal and serious administrative misconduct by the CBP workforce. In 2014 he was appointed Assistant director of the FBI for the training division in Quantanico Virginia with responsibility of overseeing policy development and delivery of all law enforcement skills and academic programs for the FBI workforce; Mark Morgan served more than 20 years with the FBI.

Peter Schweizer (422)

Peter Franz Schweizer was born November 24, 1964, is an American Political consultant and writer. He graduated from Kentridge High School and while there he attended the National Conservative Students Conference at George Washington University and was a member of Young Americans for Freedom (YAF) and a YAF alumnus speaker at the thirty fourth annual National Conservative Student Conference. Peter attended George Washington University and graduate school on YAF scholarships; he was on YAF staff starting 1993 and edited its magazine. In 2012, Schweizer and Steve Bannon co-founded the Government Accountability Institute, a Conservative think-tank whose stated goal is to investigate and expose government corruption, misuse of taxpayer money and crony capitalism; Schweizer is president of the organization; it is registered as nonpartisan but is largely focused on the Democratic Party. In 2015 he wrote the book _Clinton Cash_, in there he discussed donation made to the Clinton Foundation by Foreign entities after Bill and Hillary left the White House in 2001, it is the untold story of how and why Foreign Governments made Bill and Hillary Rich. Schweizer's early work at Senator Jeremiah Denton's National Forum Foundation (NFF), focused on the Cold War. He co-authored a National Review article with Denton's son James (Jim), "_Murdering SDI_", about the suspicious deaths of several European officials who supported the Strategic Defense Initiative. While at the NFF, Schweizer also published a report titled: "_The Meaning and Destiny of Sandinista Revolution_". In 1997 and 2005 he co-authored two novels with former Secretary of Defense Casper Weinberger. Harper Collins published _Secret Empires_, how the American Political class hides corruption and enriches family and friends. It provides details of overseas business conducted by Hunter Biden particularly in his employment with entities such as Ukranian energy firm Burisma. The book also describes ties between Elaine Chao's family business Foremost Group and China, which were disputed by a spokesman for Chao's husband, Senator Mitch McConnell. The book "was perfectly timed for the Presidential campaign" and has been cited as an initial source of the Biden Ukraine conspiracy theory. It was given significant coverage on Fox News which gained the attention of Donald Trump who sent Rudy Giuliani to Ukraine to pressure the new government to investigate the claims in Schweizer's book. In his speech at Hillsdale College on July 22, 2021   '_As a result of Biden's disastrous policy we have in just 5 months apprehended 170,000 illegal immigrants at the southern border_". Peter Schweizer lives in Tallahassee, Florida with his wife Rhonda and step-children.

Laura Ingraham (423)

Laura Anne Ingraham was born on June 19, 1963 and grew up in Glastonbury, Connecticut where she was born to Anne Caroline (Kozak), and James Frederick Ingraham III. Her maternal grandparents were Polish immigrants and her father was of Irish and English ancestry, Laura graduated from Glastonbury High School in 1981; in 1985 earned a B.A. from Dartmouth College; in 1991 she earned a Juris Doctor from the University of Virginia School of Law. In the late 1980's she worked as a speechwriter in the Reagan administration for the Domestic Policy Advisor. For a short time, she also was editor of *the Prospect*, (the magazine issued by Concerned Alumni of Princeton. Continuing with her educational pursuit in 1991 she served as a law clerk for Judge Ralph K. Winter Jr. of the US Court of Appeals for the 2nd circuit in New York and subsequently clerked for US Supreme Court Justice Clarence Thomas. After that she worked as an attorney at the New York based law firm *Skadden, Arps, Slate, Meagher and Flom*. In 1995 she appeared on the cover of the New York Times Magazine in connection with a story about young conservatives. She had three stints as a cable television host; the first was on MSNBC in the late 1990's she became a CBS commentator and hosted the MSNBC program *Watch it*. In 2001 she launched the Ingraham Show; it was heard on 306 stations, it later in 2004 moved to the talk network. In 2012 she was rated No.5 radio show in America by Talkers Magazine; In November 2012 she announced her departure from Talk Radio Network, declining to renew her contract with TRN after nearly a decade with the network. Two months earlier The Savage Nation had also left TRN. She is known as an ardent Trump supporter and was influenced by Ronald Reagan, Robert Bork, and Pat Buchanan. Several years later she hosted *Just In*, and in 2017 she became the host of a new Fox News Channel program, *The Ingraham Angle*. Following the storming of the US Capitol she was among those who advanced the theory that people associated with Antifa were responsible for the attack. In her personal life she attended a Baptist church until the age of twelve, later converting to Roman Catholicism. She has studied Russian and Spanish. In 2005 Laura announced that she had undergone treatment for breast cancer. She is a single parent with 3 children; a girl adopted from Guatemala in 2008, two boys from Russia: One adopted in 2009 and a 2nd boy adopted in 2011, every child is a child of God. She is conservative and has clearly expressed her opposition to abortion pointing out that the founder of Planned Parenthood Margaret Sanger had a disdain for the black race her ultimate goal was infanticide. About Vaccine: Her words: "I am not anti vaccine, but mandate is wrong let people make their own decision".

Kathy Ireland (424)

Kathleen Marie Ireland was born March 20, 1963 in Glendale California, the daughter of John and Barbara Ireland. At age 4 she became an independent little business lady by selling hand painted rocks, and at age 10 expanded on that; she responded to an advertisement calling for paperboys to deliver the newspapers. The person answered her call said: are you the boy asking for the job? "*No, I am not a boy, I am a girl, and can do the job just as well as any boy can and I think I deserve a chance*"; the paper agreed. Kathy got that chance and became the first ever papergirl in Santa Barbara, by the time she retired from that gig she had delivered 120,000 newspapers and was voted her district's carrier of the year for three consecutive years. With that success did she retire and collect Social Security at the old age of 19? Not quite! In 1993 Kathy Ireland's name on a line of socks sold 100 million pair and Kmart took notice subsequently giving Ireland her own clothing line including swimwear, active wear, accessories, sweaters and more. In 1993 she founded a brand marketing firm and created an excusive business relationship with Kmart, Kathy Ireland Worldwide, (or kiWW) became a global licensor, after cutting its ties to the department store chain in 2003. In 2019 her brand stood at No.26 on License Global's "Top 150 Global Licensors 2019 list with $2.6 billion in retail sales; her friend and mentor was Warren Buffett. In 2004 Kathy Ireland Worldwide was marketing products from 16 manufacturers, selling them in 34,000 retail locations in as many as 14 countries. She became a supermodel and appeared in many Television series and movies, even participated in the ninth season of *Dancing with the Stars*; she developed a close friendship with Elizabeth Taylor and publicly credits Taylor as her mentor for part of her success in life, business, design, and philanthropy. Taylor bequeathed her Jean Hersholt Humanitarian Award to Ireland, in addition to leaving her a diamond jewelry collection, which Ireland wore at the 2018 American Heart Association's "Go Red for Women Dress Show". Ireland is an ambassador for *9-1-1 For Kids*, a non-profit organization that specializes in making educational materials to assist emergency dispatchers in teaching children the proper use of 9-1-1 and other general emergency tips. In 1988 she married Greg Olsen and they have 3 children Erick, Lily and Chloe. Her sister Cynthia has a child with Down syndrome, she wrote an article about her niece and the need for an increase in research. Kathy is a devout Christian and an anti-abortion advocate and is outspoken in her support for Israel. In 2009 she appeared on Larry King Life to discuss her weight gain and women's health issues she shared that she had gained one pound a year for 25 years.

Lisa Boothe (425)

Lisa Marie Booth was born February 3, 1985 and was raised in Clifton West Virginia and claims to be an independent lady, she played all the sports available to her, such as ice skating, field hockey, lacrosse although she is a born American lady, and I am European born, now a naturalized American citizen, we seem to have all the same interests even to the point of politics, that is not all, we even celebrate our birthday on the same day, except for the fact that I am about 50 years ahead of her. She attended the University of Tennessee-Knoxville and graduated with a degree in Political science, which has helped in her career as a Republican strategist, and she is a political commentator. Lisa is currently the president of High Noon Strategies, and political communications specializing in, and navigating, crisis situations for Fortune 500 corporations. She has jumped with both feet into the political controversies that surround us on a daily basis, and is a staunch supporter of the Republican Party and President Trump. As the vice president of polling and research, she works on data driven messages for political campaigns, <u>and</u> is a network contributor on Fox News and CNN. My political pod-casts are about 5 minutes long, and hers mostly feature the full one hour, although on many of the issues we seem to think alike. Some of her articles have been criticized by the media; in an op-ed piece she wrote in 2017 while supporting US president Trump, she strongly opposed what she called Trump's continuous indignation and stated: *"Politics is a dirty industry. Many of the people criticizing him have spent plenty of time playing in the mud, they could at least wipe themselves off before handing down hypocritical moral judgments on others."* Wow, Lisa is not afraid to speak her mind and is a strong critic of the US mainstream media houses esp. of <u>the New York Times</u>, and <u>CNN</u> during, and in the wake of, US Presidential elections. In 2009 she was the assistant Press Secretary of the National Republican Congressional Committee. She has served as communications director for several US Politicians and their election campaigns. She has frequently appeared on TV debates, Boothe still young is a shrewd and provocative commentator, has touched upon many issues. She claims that her father has been a mentor and a sparring partner for her, one of her favorite hobbies was taking long walks with her mother Dianne Marie on the beach, her mom is a domestic engineer. In her media interviews she has repeatedly stated that she is a strong family girl and has close ties with her family especially with her parents and three brothers, she owns a dog named Bella, which is a Cavalier King Charles; Lisa Boothe will go far in life.

Lou Holtz (426)

Lou Holtz was born January 6, 1937 in West Virginia, the son of Anne Marie and Andrew Holtz, a bus driver. His father was of German and Irish descent, and his maternal grandparents were immigrants from Chernobyl, Ukraine. Lou grew up in Ohio, went to high school there and on to Kent State University, graduating in 1959 with a history degree then trained under Kent State's Army Reserve Officers' Training Corps and earned a commission as a Field Artillery Officer in the US Army Reserve at the time of his graduation from college. Holtz began his coaching career as a graduate assistant in 1960, at Iowa where he received his master's degree. From there he made stops as an assistant at William and Mary (1961-1963), Connecticut (1964-1965), South Carolina (1966-1967), and Ohio State (1968), there the Buckeyes football team won the national championship with Holtz as an assistant. His first job as head coach came in 1969 at William and Mary, who played in the Southern Conference at that time. In 1970 he led William and Mary to the Southern Conference title. In 1972 Holtz moved to North Carolina State University and had a 33-12-3 record in four seasons. His first three teams achieved final Top 20 rankings, including a final Top 10 finish in the 1974 Coaches Poll. His 1973 team won the ACC Championship. After 1975 he accepted an offer to leave college football and become the head coach of the NFL New York Jets. In 1977 he went to Arkansas, in 1984 he worked in Minnesota and in 1986 he took over the struggling Notre Dame, won in 1989, and won eleven of their regular season games. In 2004 Holtz announced he would retire and did so. In 2008 he was invited back to Notre Dame where a statue of Holtz was unveiled. Holtz was married to Beth Barcus till she died from cancer in 1961. He is on the Catholic Advisory board of the Ave Maria Funds and gives motivational speeches. In 2020 he endorsed Trump; he is vocal about his disapproval of Colin Kaepernick taking a knee before NFL games. Holtz is a patriot and has written 10 books; here are some of his quotes: *Ability is what you are capable of doing. Motivation determines what you do; attitude determines how well you do it. Its not the load that breaks you down, it's the way you carry it. I can't believe God put us on this earth to be ordinary. I follow 3 rules: Do the right thing, do the best you can, show people you care! He who complaints about the way the ball bounces is likely the one who dropped it. Winners embrace hard work; losers see it as punishment. In the 90's people talked about rights and privileges 25 years before they talked about obligations and responsibilities. I learn nothing by talking, learn much by listening. If you bored with life, you don't have enough goals. Life is 10% what happens to u and 90% how you respond.*

Josh Hawley (427)

Josh Hawley was born 31 December 1979 in Springdale Arkansas to banker Ronald Hawley and teacher Virginia Hawley, when Josh was two years old, they moved to Lexington, where he went to Middle School. After that to Rockhurst High School, a private Jesuit prep school in Kansas City Missouri from which he graduated in 1998 as a valedictorian; according to his middle school principal, Barbara Weibling several of his teachers thought he was probably going to be president one day. While in high school, Hawley regularly wrote columns for his hometown newspaper *The Lexington News*, writing about such topics as the American Militia Movement, following the Oklahoma City bombing, media coverage of Los Angeles Police Department detective Mark Furman, and affirmative action, which he opposed. He then studied history at Stanford University where his mother was an alumna. Hawley graduated in 2002 with a Bachelor of Arts degree with highest honors and Phi Beta Kappa membership. He studied under Professor David M. Kennedy, who later wrote the foreword to a book Hawley wrote, *Theodore Roosevelt: Preacher of Righteousness*. Kennedy said Hawley stood out in a school "which is overstuffed with overachieving and very talented young people; and has described Hawley as arguably a most gifted student, I taught in 50 years. After spending ten months in London as a post graduate intern at St Paul's School from 2002 to 2003 Hawley returned to the US to attend Yale Law School, graduating in 2006 with a Juris Doctor degree. He spent two years as a law clerk for Judge Michael W. McConnell of the US Court of Appeals for the tenth Circuit from 2006 to 2007, then for Chief Justice John Roberts of the US Supreme Court. *The Kansas City Star* reported that Hawley's classmates saw him as politically ambitious and a deeply religious conservative. While at Yale he was editor at the *Yale Law Journal* and served as president of the school's Federalist Society chapter. In June 2013 Hawley served as a faculty member of the Blackstone Legal Fellowship, which is funded by *Alliance Defending Freedom*. In 2016, Hawley ran for Attorney General of Missouri, in that position he initiated several high-profile lawsuits and investigations, including as suit against The Affordable Care Act and a suit against Governor Eric Greitens as well as an investigation in to the opioid epidemic. He is a Republican and defeated a two-term incumbent Senator in the 2018 election. In 2020 he provoked an intense political backlash when he became the first Senator to announce plans to object to the certification of Joe Biden's victory in the 2020 United States presidential election. He is a talented young senator with energy, and is just beginning, stay tune for much more to come making a difference.

Harmeet Dhillon (428)

Harmeet Kaur Dhillon was born in 1969 in Chandigarth, India. Her family moved to the United States when she was a child so that her father could pursue a career as an orthopedic surgeon. They settled in Smithfield, North Carolina, where Harmeet finished High School at age 16; after that went to Dartmouth College, there she became <u>editor-in-chief</u> at the *Dartmouth Review*. After graduating, she went on to the *University of Virginia School of Law*, where she was on the editorial board of the <u>*Virginia Law Review*</u>. After law school, she clerked for Judge Paul Victor Niemeyer of the United States Court of Appeals for the fourth circuit. Then she traveled westward and had her eyes on a political seat in the California Assembly; after a tough campaign she lost, but Harmeet was not to be deterred and tried again in 2012; it too, was unsuccessful, then served as chair of the San Francisco Republican Party. After the September 11 attacks she became a member of the ACLU. Being a fellow immigrant, I can understand her doing that, but she was heavily criticized by Republican leadership for doing that. She survived that, and became a national committee woman in 2016, even was asked to give the opening prayer at the Republican National Convention. In 2017 she was interviewed, (but not nominated) for Assistant Attorney General for Civil Rights in the Department of Justice. In 2019 Dhillon gave a speech at the President Trump Social Media Summit and was co-chair of Women for Trump; she describes Laura Ingraham as a long-time mentor. In 2017 filed a lawsuit against the University of California Berkeley, on behalf of the Berkeley College Republicans (BCR) and Young America's Foundation (YAF), for freedom of speech issues, when the school cancelled Ann Coulter's speech quoting security reasons. The suit was settled in 2018 forcing the university to change its policies about controversial speakers. In 2020 Dhillon filed suits against the State of California challenging its stay-at-home order. On behalf of two Riverside County pastors, two parishioners, seven businesses, including restaurants, a pet grooming shop, and a gondola company, she argued that their constitutional rights were being violated; she also filed suits against New Jersey and Virginia over their restriction on religious services. She criticized California for requiring the use of face mask in public, and in July 2020 she filed a lawsuit in Hawaii when the state required that visitors to Hawaii undergo quarantine upon arrival, (it is not just visitors but also for returning residents, this has seriously affected my family who have children out of state), and must endure such restrictions upon their return home, even though all are born here; a judge ruled the mandate was reasonable; Dhillen's co-council here was Jim Hochberg, who has been a very personal friend for over 50 years. Harmeet is a lady who made a major difference; her organization is Center for American Liberty, although I believe she is based in California now.

Debra M. Lewis (429)

"Defeating challenges is just a way of life" said Debra Lewis on the cover of "Midweek" October 13, 2021. Now armed with a new book and an empowering program the retired US Army Colonel is intent on showing others how they can overcome too. According to her story in Midweek she has grown into a confident battle tested coach; she assumed command of the Gulf Region as commander and district engineer, she is responsible for engineering and construction management support of deployed armed forces an Iraqi reconstruction in Baghdad and Al Anbar provinces, Iraq. The total program for Central District represents 1,400 projects valued at $2.6 billion. Colonel Lewis has commanded two previous US Army Corps of Engineers Districts. She was District Engineer for the Seattle District, Northwestern Division responsible for constructing or operating military civil/works with a staff of 850 people covering over 99.000 sq. miles in 4 states; she also served as commander of the Philadelphia District responsible for the Delaware River Basin water resource issues affecting 17 million people in 5 states. Colonel Lewis experience in command and staff positions spans over 26 years. She served on the Joint Staff in the Pentagon where she supported the JCS Chairman responsibilities for combating terrorism before and after 9/11. Other key jobs have included company command in the XVIII Airborne Corps at Fort Bragg N.C.: operations officer and executive officer of engineer battalions in Hawaii, Chief Military Engineering Division US Army Pacific (USARPAC), dealing with nations and US Territories throughout the Asia Pacific region; and staff officer in the Congressional Activities Division of the office of the Chief of staff of the Army. She was a member of the first class of women to graduate from West Point; she was the first female captain of its highly successful intercollegiate equestrian team, she was in the first class of women to complete education in the Airborne School; Her post graduate education included an MBA from the Harvard Business School, following Harvard she joined the Department of Systems engineering at West Point where she taught problem solving. She is one of the foremost coaches of Stress management, per her own statement: "I am always where trouble is". She was in the Pentagon when on September 11, 2001 a hijacked commercial airplane crashed in to the Western side of the building and it makes her an ideal coach for stress management, she said "I've faced death, faced people tried to bomb me, shoot me, kidnap me, insult me, put me down, I have had it all". Now that her and her husband have moved in to Hawaii, maybe I will get my wish one day of meeting her, looking at her picture she looks like someone you like to have as a neighbor and go for a long walk with.

Thomas Aquinas (430)

Thomas Aquinas was born the year 1225 in Roccasecca in the Kingdom of Sicily, most likely in the castle of Roccasecca that was controlled by Sicily, (present day Lazio Italy), and was the castle of his father Landulf of Acuino, a man of means who was a knight in the service of Emperor Frederick II. Landulf's brother Sinibald was abbot of Monte Cassino; the rest of the family pursued military careers and it was assumed that Thomas would follow his uncle; it would have been a normal path for a younger son of Italian nobility. At age five Thomas began his early education at Monte Cassino but was interrupted by a military conflict between Pope Gregory IX and Emperor Frederick II, it's believed that shortly thereafter Thomas was introduced to Aristotle, Averroes and Maimonides, all of whom would influence his theological philosophy. During his study in Naples, he came under influence of John of St Julian, a Dominican preacher who was recruiting followers. At age 19 he joined the Dominican Order which had been founded about 30 years earlier. His family was not pleased and his brothers seized him as he was drinking from a spring and took him back to the parent's castle. In 1879 pope Leo XIII stated that Thomas Aquinas Theology was a definitive exposition of Catholic doctrine and directed the clergy to take his teachings as the basis of their theological positions. He also decreed that all Catholic seminaries and universities must teach Thomas's doctrines, and where Thomas did not speak on a topic, teachers were urged to teach conclusions that were reconcilable with his thinking. In 1880 Saint Thomas Aquinas was declared patron of all Catholic educational establishments; his best-known works are: _Disputed Questions on Truth_ (1256-1259), _The summa Contra Gentiles_ (1259-1265), and the unfinished but massively influential _Summa Theologica, or Summa Theologiae_ (1265-1274), The Catholic Church honors Thomas Aquinas as a saint and regards him as the model teacher for those studying for the priesthood, and indeed the highest expression of both natural reason and speculative theology. The study of his works was long used as a core of the required program for those seeking ordination as priests or deacons as well as those in religious formation and for other students of the sacred disciplines such as philosophy, catholic theology, church history, liturgy, and canon law. Thomas Aquinas is considered one of the Catholic Church's greatest theologians and philosophers. He died at about age 48-49 in Fossanova, and was canonized by the Catholic Church on 18 July 1323. His remains were moved to various locations but in 1974 were returned to the home of the Dominican Order, which is the Church of the Jacobins in Toulouse France where they have remained ever since.

Betsy Ross (431)

Elizabeth Griscom Ross was born January 1, 1752 in Gloucester City, British America Colony of New Jersey. Her parents were Samuel Griscom and Rebecca James; Betsy was the eight of seventeen children of whom only nine survived childhood. She grew up in a household where plain dress and strict discipline of the Quakers dominated; she learned to sew from a great aunt, the family members had emigrated in 1680 from England. After schooling at a Quaker run state school, Betsy was apprenticed at upholsterer William Webster; there she made flags for the Pennsylvania navy during the American Revolution. After that she made US flags for over 50 years including 50 garrison flags for the US arsenal on the Schuylkill River during 1811, she was one of those hired to make flags for the Pennsylvania fleet. An entry dated May 29, 1777 in the records of the Pennsylvania Navy Board includes an order to pay her for her work as follows: "*An order on William Webb to Elizabeth Ross for fourteen pounds twelve shillings and two pence for making ships colours put into William Richards store.*" The Pennsylvania navy's ship color included an ensign, a long narrow pennant and a short narrow pennant. The ensign was a blue flag with 13 stripes, seven red stripes and six white stripes in the flag's canton (upper left-hand corner); it was flown from a pole at the rear of the ship. The long pennant had 13 vertical, red-and-white stripes near the mast; the rest was solid red; it flew from the top of the ship's mainmast, the center pole holding the sails.

Ross was one of several flag makers in Philadelphia. Betsy met Griscom while working at upholsterer William Webster; the couple eloped in 1773, marrying at Hugg's Tavern in Gloucester City, New Jersey, the marriage caused a split from her Griscom family and meant her expulsion from the Quaker congregation. The young couple soon started their own upholstery business and later joined Christ Church where there fellow congregants occasionally went included visiting colony of Virginia militia regimental commander colonel, and soon-to-be-general George Washington (of the newly organized Continental Army) and his family from their home Anglican parish of Christ Church in Alexandria Virginia, near his Mount Vernon estate on the Potomac River, along with many other visiting notaries and delegates in future years soon to be convened Continental Congress. Betsy and John Ross had no children. At the end of her life Betsy Ross was completely blind and died at age 84 on January 30, 1836. The Betsy Ross Bridge connecting Philadelphia with New Jersey across the Delaware River is named in her honor. Some have suggested that her legacy should not be about the flag, but what her story tells us is more about working women during the American Revolution.

Rick Monday (432)

Robert James "Rick" Monday was born November 20, 1945 in Arkansas; he played 19 seasons for the Kansas City/Oakland Athletes 1966-1971, Chicago Cubs (1972-1976) and Los Angel Dodgers (1977-1984). He is notable for being the first player selected in the inaugural 1965 Major League Baseball draft. In 1976 Monday prevented the flag from being burned on the field at Dodger Stadium when on April 25 two protesters ran into left center field and tried to set fire to the flag. Monday, was the Cubs center fielder, dashed over and grabbed the flag to thunderous cheers, he ran through the outfield with the flag, walked towards the Dodgers dugout, and handed the flag to pitcher Doug Rau, while security escorted the two vandals of the field. When Monday came to bat in the 5th inning, he got a standing ovation, the scoreboard behind the left field flashed this message, "RICK MONDAY.... YOU MADE A GREAT PLAY......" When Rick was asked about it later, he responded: "If you're going to burn the flag, don't do it around me, I've been to too many veterans' hospitals and seen to many broken bodies of guys who tried to protect it." Monday had served, while playing Major League Baseball, a six-year commitment with the United States Marine Corps Reserve as part of his ROTC obligation after leaving Arizona State. On August 25, 2008 Monday was presented with the American flag flown over Valley Forge National Historical Park in honor of his 1976 bicentennial flag rescue. Rick still has the flag he grabbed from the protestors that was presented to him on "_Rick Monday Day_" May 4, 1976, during a pregame ceremony at Wrigley Field by an executive of the Dodgers organization. He has been offered up to $1 million to sell it but has declined all offers. During a Dodger Stadium game on September 2, 2008, Monday was presented with a _Peace on Earth Medallion_ and _medallion lapel pin_ by Patricia Kennedy, founder of the non-profit organization _Step up 4 Vets_, for his actions. Soon in his retirement Monday became a broadcaster for the Dodgers, in 1985 by hosting the pregame show and calling play-by-play on cable TV. From 1989 to 1992 Monday moved south to call San Diego Padres games alongside Jerry Coleman; He was also a sports anchor at KTTV for a time in the 1980's, and served as a color commentator for CBS-TV at the College World Series championship game in 1988. He rejoined the Dodgers in 1993, replacing Don Drysdale, who died and played a role in the deciding game 5 of the NLCS at Olympic Stadium in Montreal; it proved to be the difference in a 2-1 Dodgers victory; Monday's home run turned out to be the Expos' only chance at a pennant in their 36-year history. Rick, 75, lives in Florida, is a member of the National College Baseball Hall of Fame, and often visits veterans in hospitals.

Tom Catena (433)

Thomas Catena was born in Amsterdam, New York as the son of an Italian-American judge, Gene Catena, and Nancy, he grew up with six siblings one of them Paul, is a Catholic priest. Tom graduated as the salutatorian from his High School and later with a bachelor's degree in mechanical engineering from Brown University in 1986. While at Brown he played with the Brown Bear football team and was a member of the Delta Phi fraternity. In 1987 he spent a year in Tokyo as an English teacher. Following that he went to Duke University where he graduated with a medical degree on a Navy scholarship. During his fourth year Catena went on his first mission to Kenya in 1992. After graduating he completed a one-year internship in internal medicine at the Naval Medical Center in San Diego in 1993 and later joined the US Navy. For the next four years he served as a flight surgeon while stationed at the Naval Support Facility Diego Garcia from 1994 to 1995. After discharge from the Navy, he did post graduate residency in family medicine at Union Hospital in Terre Haute, Indiana, while participating in one-month medical mission trips to Guyana (1997) and Honduras (1998). After that he volunteered to help the Roman Catholic Mission Board and worked in rural Kenya from 2002 – 2007 working as a consultant in Nairobi in the established Mother of Mercy Hospital in Nuba Mountains, which was built in 2007 by Bishop Macram Max Gassis and first opened in March 2008. The region has been an area of active conflict since the mid-1980 and Catena is the only surgeon for the surrounding population of 750,000 people. The hospital covers one third of South Kordofan equivalent to the size of the entire country of Austria, or the state of Maine. Patients mostly travel by foot, sometimes up to a week to reach the hospital, at any time the hospital serves between 300 and 450 patients for ailments such as fractures, diarrhea, thyroid, cancer and more and more injury from bombing attacks, or malnourishment. Humanitarian aid is restricted but Catena defies that, due to a government blockade, there are few NGOs that still operate there. Since 2012 aid is not forbidden but it is impossible to travel into most areas. Some German emergency doctors and Samaritans Purse had a presence there but there are no medical doctors in the region. Catena uses decades old treatment and engages the local community in the work as nurses and other assistive personnel. Due to bombing attacks from the past, the hospital has a number of foxholes where patients and staff can flee for the duration. Catena's is married to nurse Nasima; they have a son. He credits his faith for his work; a Muslim leader calls him Jesus Christ, always healing the sick, help the lame walk, and make the blind see; in 2018 the country honored his work and issued a postage stamp with his picture.

Desiderius Erasmus (434)

Desiderius Erasmus was born, _(exact date is in dispute)_, about 28 October 1466, in Rotterdam or Gouda the Netherlands; (*only 12 miles apart*); he was a Dutch philosopher, and is considered one of the greatest scholars of the northern Renaissance. (When I was a young boy, I thought he must have been a VIP, because the widest street in The Hague 'Den Haag' is Erasmus Straat later, I got off the tram there on my way to work.) He was a Catholic priest and an important figure in classical scholarship, who wrote in a pure Latin style. Among Humanists he has been called the crowning glory and is referred to as the prince of _Christian Humanists_ (in _my_ vocabulary that is almost an oxymoron). He was born out of wedlock, although cared for by his parents until their early death from the _black plague_ in 1483. He prepared important new Latin and Greek editions of the New Testament which raised influential questions in the Protestant Reformation and Catholic Counter Reformation. He was ordained to the Catholic priesthood on 25 April 1492, although never worked as a priest. It is rumored that he fell in love with fellow canon Servatius Rogerus and wrote many passionate letters but later distanced him self from this. He dedicated his work to Pope Leo X, as a patron of learning and regarded his work as his chief service to the cause of Christianity. All his books were published in Latin. The Protestant Reformation began in the year following the publication of his edition of the Greek New Testament (1516) and tested Erasmus's character. He chose to write in Greek and Latin which was the language of scholars thereby reaching an elite, but small, audience. He had some serious disagreements with Luther; noting Luther's contention with the Catholic Church, Erasmus had great respect for Luther and said: "It is clear that many of the Reforms for which Luther calls, are urgently needed;" and described Luther as a mighty trumpet of gospel truth. In response, Luther expressed boundless admiration for all Erasmus had done and was impressed with his superior learning. Luther hoped for his cooperation and urged him to join the Lutheran movement, but Erasmus declined and remained loyal to the church, although he criticized the riches of the popes saying it would be better for the Gospel to be _most_ important. Erasmus wrote many scholarly books on church subjects, and by 1530's his writings accounted for 10 to 20% of all book sales in Europe. While he was critical of the abuses of the Catholic Church and called for Reform, he kept his distance from Luther and continued to recognize authority of the pope emphasizing a middle path. He attempted changes within wanting Catholics to stay in the church; Erasmus died at age 69 on 12 July, 1536, while visiting Basel, and was buried there in Switzerland. A bronze statue of him was erected in his honor in Rotterdam

Mark Meadows (435)

Mark Meadows was born July 28, 1959 at a US Army hospital in Verdun France, where his father served in the Army and his mother worked as a civilian nurse. His mother was from Sevierville, Tennessee, and his father from Pineville, Arkansas. Mark grew up in Brandon Florida, and described those years as poor. He said he was a *"fat nerd"* who went on a diet after a classmate rejected him for a date. He attended Florida State University for one year from 1977-1978, and graduated from the University of South Florida with an Associate of Arts degree. In 1987 he started Aunt D's, a small restaurant in Highlands North Carolina. He sold it and used the proceeds to start a real estate development company in the Tampa Florida area. In Highlands he served as chairman of the Republican Party in Macon County and was a delegate to several state and national Republican conventions. He was on North Carolina's Board for Economic Development in Western North Carolina. In 2011, Mark moved to Glenville North Carolina, he is now the owner of Highlands Properties, which specializes in construction and land development. He got elected to the US Congress there and has an ultra-conservative voting record. He is opposed to abortion and Federal funding of abortion and although the US Supreme Court arbitrarily decided Same-Sex Marriage, Mark would vote against that. He signed the contract from America, a set of ten policies assembled by the Tea Party movement. Meadows was a founding member of the Freedom Caucus. He voted against disaster relief spending after Hurricane Sandy struck the Northeastern United States causing severe damage. He was one of several Republicans claiming the bill contained pork-barrel spending that had nothing to do with hurricane relief. Later they supported a disaster bill helping hurricane Harvey victims which caused massive damage in Louisiana ad Texas. That bill only helped storm damage victims. Meadows served as chair on government operations till 20 June, 2015. On July 28, 2015 Meadows filed a resolution to vote on removing John Boehner as speaker of the House, but it did not move forward. In the 2014 election Meadows was re-elected with 62.9% of the vote, and served as ranking member of the House Oversight Committee. After that he resigned from his congressional seat and assumed office as White House Chief of Staff In March 2020 and immediately played an influential role in the Trump administration's response to the COVID-19 Pandemic often questioning the scientific consensus on the effectiveness of face masks, while interacting with reporters Meadows refused to wear a mask, and did more; he questioned the efficacy of masks, and pressured the Food and Drug Administration to adopt less strict guidelines for COVID-19 vaccine trials.

Condoleezza Rice (436)

Condolizzaa 'Condi" Rice was born November 14, 1954 in Birmingham Alabama, the only child of Angelina and John Wesley Rice Jr. a high school guidance counselor, Presb. minister, and dean of students at Stillman College. Her name Condoleezza (in music *the term means with sweetness*). The family roots go back to pre-Civil-War days of sharecroppers and emancipation. She is 51% African, 40% European, and 9% Asian or Native American. In her 2017 book Democracy, she writes my great grandmother Zina, (*on my mother's side*), bore 5 children by different slave owners; and my great grandmother on my father's side taught her to read. When Condi grew up, the South was racially segregated. She began to learn French, music, figure skating, and ballet at age *three*, took piano lessons with the goal of becoming a concert pianist, and still loves to play. At age 15 she played Mozart with the Denver Symphony, and while Secretary of State she played regularly with a chamber group in Washington. In 1967 the family moved to Denver, where she attended St Mary's Academy, an-all-girls Catholic High School, graduated at age 16 and went to the University of Denver where her father was assistant dean. She majored in music, but considered an alternate major of International Politics. In 1974 at age 19 Rice was inducted into the Phi Beta Kappa Society and was awarded a BA cum Laude in Political Science by the University of Denver. She then got a Masters in Political Science at Notre Dame in 1975 and in 1977 went to work at the State Department during the Carter Administration. In 1979 she studied Russian at Moscow State University. At age 26 she received her Ph. D in Political Science at the University of Denver; her dissertation centered on military policy in Czechoslovakia. From 1980 to 1981 she was a Fellow at Stanford University Arms Control and Disarmament Program, having won a Ford Foundation Dual Expertise Fellowship in Soviet Studies and International Security. Till 1982 Condi was a Democrat and disagreed with the foreign policy of jimmy Carter and changed to Republican. She was a specialist on the Soviet Union at Berkeley. In 2005 she became the 66th US Secretary of State, played an important role in trying to stop the nuclear threat from North Korea. In 1985 North Korea had signed the Nuclear Non-Proliferation Treaty, but in 2002 they were operating secret nuclear weapons. Rice was strong to have North Korea suspend their nuclear program. In 1986 Rice served as special assistant to the director of the Joint Chiefs of Staff. When she was confirmed as Secretary of State, she pioneered Transformational Diplomacy directed toward expanding the number of responsible democratic governments in the world and especially in the Greater Middle East. To do justice to Condi Rice we need a 1000-page book.

Louise (437)

Princess Louise, Carolina Alberta, was born 18 March 1848 and was the fourth daughter and sixth child of Queen Victoria and Prince Albert. She was brought up with the strict education program of Queen Victoria. Louise was a talented and intelligent child, and attended art school. When her father died in December 1861 the court went into a long period of mourning. Louise was an able sculptor and artist. Before her marriage she served as an unofficial secretary to the Queen from 1866 to 1871. The question of Louise's marriage was discussed, and suitors were suggested but Victoria did not want her to marry a foreign prince; Louise fell in love with John Campbell, the Duke of Argyll. Victoria approved the marriage on 21 March 1871. After a happy beginning, the two drifted apart, possibly because of their childlessness and the Queen's constraint on their activities. The Royal couple moved to Canada, there her husband represented the Queen and attend the opening of Parliament. In later years her husband died on 2 May, 1914, and Louise moved back to England and on December 3, 1939 at the age of 91 she died. The province of Alberta in Canada was named after her. Some years ago, we visited Canada, picked up our rental car in Calgary and began our 3-day journey. As we were excited traveling Calgary on *Trans-Canada highway* #1, we traveled the 127 km to Banff and every mile is breathtaking scenic beauty with glacier fed rivers along side and these majestic snow-covered mountains the beauty began as soon as we left Calgary. The Canadian Rockies are the worlds greatest material marvels the total distance to Lake Louise is 182 km and with the immaculate road of Trans Canada Hwy I the trip could be accomplished in 2 hours but being photo enthusiast, we decided to make the trip in 4 days. The landscape to Banff is constantly changing as we traveled alongside Glacier fed-rivers, some flowing in the aqua marine waters in the Rocky Mountain lakes. We had booked a room at the Fairmont Banff Springs Hotel for our first overnight stay, it is a totally renovated hotel originally owned and built in 1880 by the Canadian Pacific Railway; one day in Banff is not enough; two days later we drove the remainder of the 182 km along Trans Canada Hwy 1. The final destination being *Lake Louise*, world famous for its turquoise lake the Victoria Glacier, which is a site that cannot be described but must be seen with its colored, glacier fed water in to a lake, named after a princess. When we first saw that magnificent site nestled between snow-covered mountains what cane to mind was; if this lake, "as well as the province" is named after a princess, she must have been a very beautiful lady. We did not know at first that Louise was the daughter of the renowned Queen Victoria, but in the words of the late Paul Harvey: "*Now you know the rest of the story*."

Ariana (438)

We are not sure if her family is out, therefore we have changed her name to Ariana. She grew up under the oppressive Iranian regime for the first nine years of her life, born into a Christian family. Dad was a defense attorney and Christian pastor, quite challenging in Iran. "I had everything but we were never truly safe." In 2009 the government persecuted Christians and clamped down on all Christian activity. People were arrested, our phones were tapped and we were secretly followed. We were heartbroken and frightened. Our family moved to another country; my introduction to conservatism resulted from my family's flight for religious freedom. Now living in America, religious liberty is what I am passionate about. Here I realized I have rights I never knew I had. In Iran we can not protect ourselves, a firearm is illegal, here in America with the 2nd amendment we have right to defend ourselves. In high school I am president of the ethics club and as students we can challenge ethical issues, even challenge our teachers; I could never imagine this in Iran. College has been very different, many of my peers embrace leftist ideas I decided to join a conservative group, but to my surprise there was none. My classes were indoctrination centers with only far left ideas. My political science classes may well be professors from Iran, it's the same. Don't these professors understand they are not teaching, but are indoctrinating liberal philosophy, don't they understand in America our God given rights are enshrined in the Constitution? There was no conservative professor and I felt alone. Then things changed...I discovered Young America's Foundation (YAF); we met on social media, decided to organize a YAF chapter meet on campus. In a year, it grew from 7 to 70 students sharing ideas. We are growing daily and just had a retreat...wow. For the first time I have peers in school standing up for conservative ideas. The time we are together is precious. We can freely speak on issues like abortion, BLM movement, and the 2nd amendment. Some professors have spoken secretly about their ideas but there are almost no faculty with such ideas, if they attend, they want to come in secret. It breaks my heart that some professors can not speak freely about conservative issues, this is America. I am an Iranian/American and professors just assume that I am liberal. It leaves me speechless that they are stunned when they discover I am conservative. After graduating I want to go to law school and become a defence attorney. The American legal system is the best in the world. YAF has opened my eyes and inspired me, I still have a hard time believing I am really here living in a free country. Why do people here want to go back to what I left behind? I am totally confused.

Alice Ball (439)

Alice Augusta Ball was born July 24, 1892 in Seattle Washington, to James Pressley and Laura Louise Howard Ball. She was one of four children. Her family was middle class and well off, as her father was a newspaper editor of the *Colored Citizen*, photographer and lawyer, her mother also worked as photographer. Her grandfather James Ball Sr. was a photographer and one of the first black Americans to make use of daguerreotypy, (the process of printing photographs on metal plates). Some researchers have suggested that her parents' and grandfather's love for photography may have played a role in her love for chemistry, as they worked with mercury vapors and iodine sensitized silver plates to develop photos. Despite being prominent members and advocates of the African American community, both of Ball's parents are listed as "White" on her birth certificate. This may have been an attempt to reduce the prejudice and racism their daughter would face and help her "pass" in white society. The family moved from Seattle to Honolulu in 1903 in hopes that the warm weather would relieve her grandfather's arthritis. He died shortly after the move and in 1905 they re-located back to Seattle after only one year in Hawaii. Alice attended Seattle High School, achieved top grades in the sciences, graduated in 1910, and continued further study in chemistry at the University of Washington earning a bachelor's degree in pharmaceutical and chemistry in 1912 and a second one in 1914, and published a 10-page article "*Benzoylations in Ether solution*," in the journal of the American Chemical Society. (Publishing an article in a respected scientific journal was an uncommon accomplishment for a woman and especially for a black woman at that time. She was offered many scholarships but decided to take the college of Hawaii, (now the university of Hawaii.) and went there to research the chemical makeup of plants and studied chaulmoogra oil and its chemical properties. It had been the best treatment available for leprosy for hundreds of years, and Ball developed a much more effective injectable form. In 1915 she became the first woman and the first black American to graduate with a master's degree from the College of Hawaii; she was also the first African American research chemist *and* instructor in the College of Hawaii's chemistry department. At that time people diagnosed with leprosy were exiled to Molokai with the expectation that they would die there. Her technique would make the oil imjectionable and absorbable by the body. Before she could publish her findings, Ball became ill and returned to Seattle for treatment; but it was not successful, and on December 31, 1916 at her young age of 24 she died. Her death certificate lists the cause as unknown.

Patricia Bath (440)

Patricia Era Bath was born Nov. 4, 1942 in New York City to Rupert and Gladys Bath, her father was an immigrant from Trinidad, a newspaper columnist, and first black man to work for the NY City Subway as a motorman, and inspired her love for cultures; her mother was descended from African slaves and Cherokee Native Americans, and helped pay for her children's education. He parents often told her to never settle for less than her best and encouraged her to pursue her dreams and love for science, and bought her the first chemistry set. In high school she was inspired by Albert Schweitzer's work in medicine; and applied for and won a National Science Foundation Scholarship. This led to her cancer research earning a front-page feature in the New York Times. She was led to research the connections between cancer, nutrition and stress, her discoveries were published and at age 18 were shared at the international fifth congress of nutrition in 1960. She received her Bachelor of Arts in chemistry from Manhattan's Hunter College in 1964, and transferred to Howard University College of Medicine, there she was awarded a scholarship to Yugoslavia where she focused on research in pediatric surgery. She graduated from Howard and was awarded an excellence in Ophthalmology. The assassination of Martin Luther King Jr. in 1968, dedicated her to achieve the dream of King, and returned to intern at Harlem hospital center, now affiliated with Columbia University College of Physicians and Surgeons. There she saw a large number of blind people, and began collecting data on visual impairment and did her first eye surgery in 1969 while serving her residency in ophthalmology, the first African American to do so, there she discovered that blacks have eight times higher prevalence of glaucoma a cause for blindness. She has been credited with bringing community ophthalmology as a new discipline in medicine promoting eye health and blindness prevention through programs utilizing methodologies in public health, especially to underserved populations. Bath's main humanitarian efforts are through her work at the American Institute for the Prevention of Blindness co founded with others one them being Nigerian born Aaron Ifekwunigwe a pediatrician and human rights advocate. Bath was able to travel and spread eye care throughout the globe by providing newborns with free eye drops, vitamins and malnourishment vaccinations against diseases that can cause blindness. In her travels she did laser cataract surgery and coined the term "Laserphaco Probe" short for Photo Ablative Cataract Surgery. She holds five patents in the US. and has been a pioneer in the prevention of blindness. Patricia Bath died of cancer at age 76 on May 30, 2019 at the University of California medical center.

Yvonne Clark (441)

Georgiana Yvonne Young was born April 13, 1929 in Houston Texas. Her father, Dr Coleman Milton Young Jr. was a physician surgeon and her mother Hortense Houston Young was a librarian and journalist the Louisville Defender. As a child she had a love for finding and fixing things, but was not allowed to take a mechanical drawing class at school because she was a girl. She took an aeronautics class in high school and joined the school's Civil Air Patrol where she learned to shoot and had flying lesson in a simulator. In 1945 she graduated from high school at age 16 and spent the next 2 years at Girls Latin School in Boston. She then became the first woman to earn a degree in mechanical engineering from Howard University, where she was a cheerleader and the only female in her class of almost entirely returned World War II veterans. After she graduated in 1951, she got more surprises, and discovered that the engineering job market was not very receptive to women, particularly women of color. She was the first African American woman to earn a masters degree in engineering management from Vanderbilt University in 1972; her thesis was titled: "*Designing procedures for materials flow management in major rebuild projects in the glass industry*" Her first job after getting her degree was in the Frankford Arsenal Gauge Lab, a US Army ammunition plant in Philadelphia. After that she moved to a small record label, RCA Camden in New Jersey, where she designed factory equipment. She returned to the South to get married, and married William F Clark Jr. a bio chemistry teacher at Meharry Medical College in 1955. They had a son in 1956 and a daughter in 1968. She became the first female member of the Tennessee State University mechanical engineering department, joining the faculty in 1956. She twice chaired the department, initially from 1965 until 1970, and then starting in 1977 she held the position for 11 years, after that she retired as a professor. She helped to start the Tennessee State chapter of *Pi Tau Sigma*, a mechanical engineering society. She made great efforts to encourage women to become engineers and reported in 1997 that 25% of the students in her department were female. She also worked at NASA, Westinghouse, and Ford. She spent many summers working with NASA there she helped design the containers Neil Armstrong used to bring moon samples back to earth. Yvonne was the main investigator for the research project "*Experimental Evaluation of the Performance of Alternative Refrigerants in Heat Pump Cycles*" funded by the Department of Energy Oak Ridge National Laboratory. She was the student division team leader for the NASA funded project. Yvonne Clark died at age 89 on January 27, 2019 in Nashville Tennessee.

Victor Orban (442)

Victor Mihaly Orban was born 31 May, 1963 in Szekesfehervar, Hungary, and grew up in a rural middle-class family as the eldest son of the entrepreneur and agronomist Gyozo Orban and special educator and speech therapist Erzsebet Sipos. His paternal grandfather Mihaly Orban practiced farming and animal husbandry. Orban spent his childhood in two nearby villages Alcsutdoboz and in Vertesacsa. In 1977, his family moved permanently to Szekesfehervar. Orban graduated from Blanka Teleki High School in Szekesfehervar in 1981 where he studied English. After completing two years of military service, he studied law at Eotvos Lorand University in Budapest, writing his master's thesis about the Polish Solidarity movement. After graduation in 1987 he lived in Szolnok for two years, commuting to his job in Budapest at the Management Training Institute of the Ministry of Agriculture and Food. Orban married jurist Aniko Levai in 1986; the couple have five children. Orban is a member of the Calvinist Hungarian Reformed Church, while his wife and their five children are Roman Catholic. His critics include Hillary Clinton, Angela Merkel, and the presidents of the European Commission Jose Manuel Barroso, and Jean-Claude Juncker, intergovernmental and non-governmental organizations, and Hungarian-American business magnate and political activist George Soros with whom Orban for some time has been involved in a personal war. Why are we featuring him here? He has been accused of pursuing anti democratic reforms, attacking human rights of LGBT people, reducing the independence of Hungary's press, judiciary, central bank, and lastly but not least, he has reduced cronyism and nepotism. In spite of all the criticism he ran a successful campaign and got twice re-elected to be the Hungarian Prime Minister and has been the successful leader of Hungary since 2010, while presiding over Fidesz, a national conservative political party for some time, perhaps as far back as the mid 1990's. Being European born myself, I have followed him from a distance for sometime. And believe that he is, or may be the first post- "Cold-War" head of government in Eastern and Central Europe who has not been a member of the Soviet era communist regime. Orban became a founding member of the Anticommunist Federation of Young Democrats (FIDESZ), and has become their leader, winning 14 of Hungary's 22 seats in the European Parliament; there is no question about the fact that Hungary is still struggling economically, but it is on the right course now. In his first year as prime minister he pushed through a series of broad legislative measures that culminated in the adoption of a new constitution. Largely in response to foreign criticism his government was forced to scale back, being accused of getting too much power over the press. Despite all the criticism and opposition, the election results seem to re-affirm strong support for Orban's leadership, he has allowed job creations, has been supportive of working families and asserted Hungarian interests internationally. From the early years the Orban government has criticized George Soros, as well as his NGOs in particular for his support for more open immigration similar to what the Democratic Party is inflicting on America right now. Orban has appointed a number of young ministers who have not been associated with previous governments, and took steps to move the country toward a free-market economy. The Israeli ambassador initially joined the chorus but changed just before the official visit of Netanyahu to Hungary. In my opinion it is a plus to be criticized and not liked by George Soros. Victor Orban may not have reached sainthood yet, but the very fact that he has been re-elected twice by his own people is an indication that he has earned a place on these pages.

Mollie Hemingway (443)

Mollie Ziegler Hemingway was born August 3, 1974 in Denver Colorado; her parents are Larry and Carolyn Ziegler, he is a retired Missouri Synod Lutheran pastor and her mother was a school teacher. Mollie went to Douglas County High School, then got her bachelors degree in economics at the University of Colorado and is an American conservative author, columnist and political commentator, having been a fan of her for a long time she is a good one. She is the recipient of the Young Conservative Leadership "Buckley Award." I love the story how Mollie made coffee at a Spanish Language Trade Publication and was given a chance to write a story, she did, and was hooked; Mollie has kept her personal and home background very private and rightfully so. She is married and has two children, and is not afraid to step into controversy and at one time she was rather critical of Trump, but what is one of her strong areas is that she is willing to change when she sees the truth. Trump is a flawed person (like we all are), but he led the country in a positive direction and Mollie saw that too. She is the editor in chief of *The Federalist* (*American Conservative on line magazine and podcast that covers politics, policy, culture and religion*". She has written several books and in October 2021 she released a new book "*Rigged*"); I have that on order. Apparently, Mollie dares to put in print what most of us are thinking. "If you are questioning how Biden got into the Whitehouse and how the media and big tech duped America, according to Mollie, then you are not wrong. *Mollie you are my hero*, I hope your book becomes a top seller in America, please keep talking. Rather than accept Trump won and Clinton lost; the political and media establishment desperately explained away Trump's victory. They settled on a destructive four-year conspiracy theory that crippled the government, empowered America's adversaries and illegally targeted private innocent citizens whose only crime was not supporting Hillary Clinton. The Russia collusion hoax had all the elements of a conspiracy theory including baseless claims of hacked voting totals, illegal voter suppression, and treasonous collaboration with a foreign power. Pundits and officials speculated openly that President Trump was a foreign asset and members of his circle were under the thumb of the Kremlin. Despite the patent absurdity of these claims, the belief that Trump stole the 2016 election had the support of the most powerful institutions and individuals. "I know he's an illegitimate president," Clinton claimed of Trump. Jimmy Carter said: "Trump did not actually win...the Russians put him there". Mueller ran a multi-year and a multi-million-dollar investigation and found no evidence. Mollie, you said what we all know to be so. If you make it to Hawaii, I love to share a cappuccino with you in person.

Alfred Vogel (444)

Alfred Vogel was born 26 October 1902, in Aesch, Basel, Switzerland and was a Swiss herbalist, naturopath and writer. At the age of 21 he began to manage a health store. In 1927, he married Sophie Sommer; together they had two daughters. In 1929 he began publishing a monthly magazine <u>Das Neue Leben</u>, (The new life), and in 1941 he titled it <u>Gesundheits-Nachrichten</u> (health news. In Northern Europe where my family lived during the 1940's with no heating in the homes it was often cold and damp in our home, and for my parents it was the time that arthritis and rheumatism was playing havoc with their bodies. Advice from the family physician was live with it. But Vogel had many natural remedies so much so that his magazine or newsletter was like Gospel to someone like my father; their bodies and joints in that climate was keeping them from living a full life; it was in those years that my parents nearly lived a died by the medical information from Dr. Vogel; he may not have been a doctor but in our home, he was doctor Vogel. He was an avid traveler and enjoyed visiting new countries and new cultures, and had great interest in meeting indigenous people who lived in close relationship with nature. In the 1950's he traveled extensively through Africa, North and South America and Oceania. On one of his travels in the United States he met, and stayed with, the Sioux native American tribe and befriended Ben Black Elk, son of medicine man Nicholas Black Elk, who Vogel said taught him about Native American herbal tradition. However, Ben Black Elk was known to earn his bread with taking pictures of him with tourists near Mount Rushmore for money. When Vogel departed Ben Black Elk gave him a farewell present: *a handful of seeds of Echinacea purpurea* (purple coneflower). Back in Switzerland Vogel began cultivating and researching the plant, eventually creating Echinaforce, that would become his flagship product. He continued throughout his life search remote areas, while traveling the globe. In Europe he continued to publish his newsletter in there he championed the use of natural remedies in healthcare and has contributed to increased recognition of the distinct role herbal medicine can play in the modern world we live in. He may not have been a medical doctor with an MD degree but he helped many people living a more healthy and productive life. His quest to understand how plants can be used as medicines and to find effective herbal-based remedies was his motivation to explore nature and the world at large, Alfred Vogel never stopped his pursuit in discovering the relationship plants have on living a life we can also enjoy. He lived till age 93 and died October 1 1996 in Feusisberg Switzerland.

Trischa Zorn (445)

Trischa Zorn was born June 1, 1964 in Arnhem Netherlands with Aniridia, which is a congenital eye condition caused by dysfunction in the PAX6 gene, (the gene responsible for eye development); it causes the eye to stop developing prematurely. The only treatment is surgery involving a synthetic iris replacement, which reduces the amount of light entering the eyes. Before she received the surgery, she could only see objects that were a few feet in front of her. After the surgery her vision improved from 20/1100 to 20/850. The surgery's main purpose was to help cut down glare from light coming in to her eyes. Tricia was an athlete and because she was partially blind, she qualified for the Paralympics Games from 1980 and so far, has collected 55 medals, (41 gold, 9 silver, and 5 bronze), and broken 8 world records at the Paralympics in swimming, and has raised the bar for Paralympics athletes. In her first games in 1980, she won seven gold medals and collected several more throughout the years. At the 1992 games in Barcelona, she topped the individual medal table with ten gold medals and two silver, and won more medals than any other athlete; although she is an accomplished athlete while discussing her accomplishments in London in 2012, she aired her frustration with the classification system that has disadvantaged some United States swimmers because of what she sees as its subjective nature. She also talked about increased visibility of the Games, how things have changed from when she started in 1980 to the 2012 Summer Paralympics. Zorn discussed how sponsorship has evolved from her early time participating and issues with the Paralympics inside the United States at the present. This year Zorn was inducted into the International Paralympics Hall of Fame at a ceremony in London. Having last competed in the 2004 Summer Paralympics, if she was swimming today, she would be classified as an S12 swimmer (*classification based on their disability*). She currently works for the United States Department of Veterans Affairs, helping returning soldiers adjust to life as civilians. She had studied Special Education at the University of Nebraska and school administration and supervision at Indiana University-Purdue University Indianapolis and law at the IU Robert H. Mc Kinney School of Law. On January 1, 2005 Zorn was one of eight athletes honored during New Year celebration in Times Square in New York City, some of the others were from Australia, Liberia, Cameroon, Dominican Republic, China and US. The athletes were center stage during the festivities in the countdown leading up to ringing in the New Year. In 2012 Zorn was inducted in to the International Paralympics Hall of Fame.

Mae Jemison (446)

Mae Carol Jemison was born October 17, 1956 in Decatur, Alabama US, the youngest of three children of Charlie and Dorothy Jemison. Her father was a maintenance supervisor for a charity organization and her mother worked most of her career as an elementary school teacher of English and Math at the Ludwig van Beethoven Elementary school in Chicago Illinois. The family first lived in Woodlawn and later in the Morgan Park neighborhood. Mae always knew what she wanted to do from very young and told her kindergarten teacher she wanted to be a scientist when she grew up, the teacher interpreted that she wanted to be a nurse. Women (especially black women in science was not common; she said later in the 50's and 60's when everyone was excited and thrilled about space, I was irritated not seeing any females in the space program there were no women astronauts. She studied ballet at age 8 and 9 and at age 12 entered high school and had aspirations of becoming a professional dancer. At age 14 she auditioned for the leading role of Maria in West Side Story; she did not get it but was selected as a background dancer. She graduated from Chicago's Morgan Park High School in 1973 and at age 16 entered Stanford University. There were very few African American students in her class but it did not faze her she said: I was young, naïve and stubborn but continually experienced discrimination from her teachers. She later said in a newspaper interview, my youth and arrogance may have helped me to function in a white male-dominated society; at Stanford she was head of the Black Students Union. During her senior year she vacillated between medical schools or pursue a career as professional dancer. In 1977 she graduated receiving a B.S. degree in chemical engineering and a B.A. in African American studies. While at Stanford she never gave up on her childhood dreams of going into space and considered applying to NASA. She attended Cornell Medical School and during her training went on a study tour to Cuba, and worked later at a Cambodian refugee camp; after that was stationed in East Africa working for Flying Doctors. In 1981 she graduated from Cornell with an M.D. degree and interned at Los Angeles USC Medical Center in 1982 as a general practitioner. In 1983 she worked in the Peace Corps in Liberia and Sierra Leone. Upon her return to the US, she worked in private practice, took engineering courses and applied for NASA training and worked in shuttle verification computer software in the Shuttle Avionics Integration Laboratory (SAIL); in addition to her MD degree, she holds many honorary doctorates and in 1993 was inducted in the National Women's Hall of Fame, and the International Space Hall of Fame.

Tom De Meester (447)

Tom R. De Meester was born March 7, 1938 in Grand Rapids Michigan. In 1958 he married Carol Walburg and together they have 4 children, Steven, Sara, Scott, and Susan. Tom went to Calvin College graduating in 1959 with a BA degree, then to the University of Michigan graduating with his MD in 1963, and onto Johns Hopkins Hospital in Baltimore; working as a surgical intern; following that, returned to the Univ. of Michigan and worked with Dr C. Gardner Child III as surgical assistant resident. The family has been very personal friends since early 1970's while they lived in Hawaii, where Tom was assistant chief of Thoracic-Cardiovascular Surgery at Tripler Army Medical Center during the 1970's. It was at that time that we met Tom and Carol at church and developed a personal friendship. Tom and I had very different interests, he was dedicated to the medical profession and my interest was business and political. We were both Evangelical Christians and developed a long friendship that endured through the years. After they moved away to Chicago where Tom was professor of Thoracic surgery at the University of Chicago; Pritzker School of Medicine, (Pritzker was one of the wealthiest Jewish charity-oriented Americans). There I enjoyed a rest-stop in Chicago visiting them on my way back from Washington DC. On one of these stops Tom came to the airport and said: *"Terry I have an emergency heart surgery and can not leave; you have 2 choices: go home to Carol and rest, or stay with me and watch while I do this open-heart surgery."* The choice was not hard, when would I ever have an opportunity to watch an open-heart surgery? I submitted to a scrub and the next thing I stood left of Tom; opposed to us were 2 students Tom was teaching and at the head was the same process with the anesthesiologist. When Tom made the first cut, I will confess I got a little woozy, but after that I received an education to see an experienced surgeon at work with great ease making skillful cuts opening the body until he reached the tumor, cut it out, have the lab test it immediately, and then begin the process of putting the body back the way it was. I said to Tom: "This man will be sick." He said: "No Terry in a few hours he will be walking." After that I made many more stops. Tom De Meester was an accomplished surgeon with degrees and honors that would fill this book. Even Linkoping University of Sweden honored him twice with an honorary doctorate. The studies of Dr Tom De Meester have resulted in almost 500 publications in peer reviewed journals, 175 book chapters and 9 books, his contributions to understanding to patho-physiology of diseases of the esophagus and their surgical correction and treatment of cancer has resulted in 43 lectures around the world. How did a simple man like me get so blest to call a VIP like Tom De Meester my personal friend?

Ronald Dion DeSantis (448)

Ronald Dion DeSantis was born on September 14, 1978, in Florida, the son of Karen Rogers and Ronald DeSantis, of Italian descent; the family moved to Orlando when Ron was six years old. While they lived in Dunedin, he was a member of the Little League team that made it to the Little League World Series in Williamsport Pennsylvania. After graduating from Dunedin high school, he attended Yale University, there was captain of Yale's varsity baseball team and joined the Delta Kappa Epsilon fraternity, one of the oldest fraternities in the US Founded in 1844. In December of 2017 Trump said if DeSantis should run for governor, he would support him; in January 2018 DeSantis announced his candidacy for governor of Florida. The Republican governor Rick Scott was term limited. DeSantis supported Trump, running an ad "*Make America Great Again*." The leftist media then tried to muddy the campaign with racist issues. DeSantis had made a comment: "*The last thing we need is to monkey this up by trying to embrace a Socialist agenda with huge tax increases*". He was accused of using the verb "*monkey*" as a racist dog whistle, his opponent was African-American. The words received widespread media coverage and the issue became unstoppable. Today's media mostly consists of young reporters, who echo each other. DeSantis took Jeanette Nunez a Latina as his running mate, who served in the Florida House of Representatives, and they focused full attention on the gubernatorial campaign, the media accused him of having no policy platform. He put one together and was endorsed by the Florida Police Chief Association. His opponent was Andrew Gillum, who had served as a City Commissioner and 126th mayor of Tallahassee. The race was tight and so was the vote of November 6, 2018, it was DeSantis 49.6% and Gillum 49.2%. After a careful recount DeSantis was declared the winner with 0.4%, the closest ever in such election; Gillum conceded on November 17. He has been a successful governor and great supporter of the Republican agenda, although the Democratic leadership halted the wall and widely opened the borders to immigrants many of whom have no intention on shedding their ethnic attrition, meaning they often do not intent to assimilate. That was not so in the 1950's when we as Europeans arrived. There was no welfare for the immigrant, we went to English Schools and were forced to survive in the new world with no other choice. Many were required to have sponsors who would guarantee help. It was tough but *that* made America great. Open borders will attract the worlds poorest people and is unfair to those who waited in line. DeSantis is one of those European immigrant descendents, that will make America great and would make a great president.

Richard R. Kelley (449)

Dr Richard R. Kelley has made profound contributions to developing Hawaii's visitor industry, helping to bring the world to Hawaii. He got his start in the world of tourism. Before Richard Kelley helped grow Outrigger Hotels into a multinational hospitality chain he worked as a pathologist at the Queens hospital in the 1960's. Even though he was a busy man, he always found time to engage in a conversation with anyone he came in contact with. Body tissues and fluids and diseases in general he knew, but he had a most valuable asset and that was getting to know people. "Best part of my job was getting to know patients, nurses" he was no ordinary doctor; he listened and respected every person he met. He said his days in medicine were short lived after his parents convinced him to give up medicine and begin working in the hotel industry. The family had just acquired the Prince Kuhio Hotel and all of a sudden, we had about 400 employees. I did not want to lose the friendship and closeness I had with the people. We had a quarterly newsletter which soon became weekly. From 1984 till 2016 when the family sold the business, he estimates we generated about 1650 such newsletters, it was when the head of the company talks directly to the employees. He never lost that personal touch with his workers; he said: "I made it a point to go down to housekeeping in the morning and have a cup of coffee with the housekeepers, and they'd begin asking me questions, and I would ask them questions too, its how we got to know each other much better. We had mutual respect for each other, and hope we never lose that in business. If you treat your employees well, you find that they treat you well they'll treat the company well and treat the community well. That was the attitude of the CEO of the Outrigger Hotels. His memoirs and business tutorial have been assembled in his book about to be published *Paddling the Outrigger*, pulls together Kelley's thoughts on a variety of topics including his birth and upbringing in Waikiki, the book will get launched in November 2021. He was interviewed by Mossman of Midweek who published the story in the October 27 issue. Although Dr Kelly credits David Carey for the Hotel success, when they opened in the 1940's, a room was rented for $7.50 a night. Dr Kelley got his start in the 1940's working at his parent's hotel. It is now a growing hotel chain throughout the Pacific operating 12,000 hotel rooms and condominium units in more than 50 properties from Waikiki to Moololaba on the Sunshine Coast Region of Queensland Australia. The Kelley Family was my client and owned homes on the beach at Diamondhead. I was often invited there for morning coffee and have pleasant memories of my visits with family members. I met Dr Kelley only one time, we spoke briefly.

Sarah Huckabee Sanders (450)

Sarah E. Huckabee was born Aug. 13, 1982 in Hope Arkansas, the youngest child and only daughter of Mike and Janet Huckabee; she has two brothers John Mark and David. Following graduation of Little Rock High School and on to Ouachita Baptist University Sarah was elected student body president, in addition to her studies she was active in the Republican Party and was majored in Political Science and minored in Mass Communication, graduating with a Bachelor of Arts degree. In 2010 she married Bryan Sanders and they have 3 children. She introduced herself this way: "I'm Sarah Huckabee Sanders, a proud Christian conservative mom, an "*America First*" patriot, former White House Press Secretary for President Trump, and right now a candidate to be the next Governor of Arkansas. Together we must stand up to the Biden-Harris left wing agenda. She was involved in her fathers Senate and Governor Campaign. He lost some but became the governor of Arkansas; now Sarah has a strong desire to sit in her father's chair, and feels competent that she is up to the challenge. Former President Trump has pledged support for his former Press Secretary. She has already pledged her support for closing the Southern border, Upholding the ban on Sanctuary Cities, expressed strong support for the police, and standing up for America. These issues would have received near 100% support from every sane American only a few years ago. But now the Democratic Party is hell bent on destroying the country, a situation we have never seen before. Just 50 years ago we had a press and it was still possible to get to hear two sides of the prevailing issues; but unfortunately, America has lost that. The media has closed ranks behind the Democratic Party and people like Sarah need deliver her own message. Of course, there are no winners till people have voted, but looking at the Remington Research group their data shows that Sarah may secure her wish; she is viewed favorable by 78% of Republican voters with a 57-point lead. Having chaired many such campaigns we all know that no election is settled until the day after the ballots are cast, and the count is certified. Her *opponent* comes in at 11% and the *no opinion* also at 11%, although I am reminded of the Colloquialism "*It ain't over till the fat lady sings*", which I believe was credited to Ralph Carpenter in the Dallas Morning News when he commented on a basketball score of the previous day that was tied at press time. Those of us who have ran or helped to get our favorite candidate elected, know the reality behind such a comment. Irrespective of your political conviction Sarah Huckabee is a mother of 3 children and to endure such a political campaign should be commended for courage and bravery and my comment to her is: God bless you, Sarah! You need His blessings to win, and to execute the required tasks after you win.

Julia Coleman (451)

Julia Coleman was born December 19, 1991 in Maplewood Minnesota and graduated from the University of Minnesota, Twin Cities. Being the daughter of a law enforcement officer, she grew up with conservative principles such as; the rule of Law, Limited Government, and Individual Liberty. In College she attended a Leadership Institute seminar, and found it a conservative boot camp training that taught the same principles she had been raised with in the home, therefore they stuck with her through college… At the University of Minnesota, she witnessed the campus left's intimidation and indoctrination firsthand. Julia demonstrated strong interest in politics and public service. She studied political science and held internships with the Minnesota State Senate, which would serve her well later on. The youth leadership seminar interested Julia so much she followed up and attended another one later in her own words: "I learned so much." After she graduated from college, she wanted to help the conservative movement in a big way. She traveled to the LI headquarters in Arlington Virginia and took the rigorous field representative training and begin to understand more and more the value of helping other young conservatives stand up for their principles on campus. Her performance impressed the Institute staff, who hired her as a field representative for Delaware and New Jersey, in that work she gained tremendous experience organizing conservative students, assisting them with their projects and mentoring them. She helped them set up powerful visual demonstrations for their viewpoints such as Criminals for Gun Free Zones pointing out humorously the folly of leftists pushing for anti-gun laws. After several months she returned to Minnesota. In 2018 she married Jacob and now has three young sons, including newborn twins. With all that training Julia felt prompted to seek elective office and did so. She ran and won at age 29, and was sworn in as the youngest female state senator representing the 47th district in the state of Minnesota ever elected. Her victory gave the Senate a Republican majority, but it did not come without trials; her pregnancy had complications and the doctor recommended she abort one of the babies; but with her strong Catholic faith and conservative principles Julia refused and gave birth to two healthy boys. She now is a State Senator and champions her steadfast conservative pro-life views as a Minnesota State Senator. Julia said: "You look at life a lot differently when you realize you are raising children in today's society. I rolled up my sleeves and was proud to fight for the future of my children. Julia Coleman wanted to make a difference and did so in a big way; for her it meant stop talking, act, and get involved.

John Fund (452)

John H. Fund was born April 8, 1957 in Tucson Arizona; he attended California State University in Sacramento and studied journalism, and economics; after graduating he worked as a research analyst for the California State Legislature in Sacramento before beginning his journalism career in 1982 as a reporter for the syndicated columnists Rowland Evans, and Robert Novak. In 1993, he went on to the Wall Street Journal for two decades, and wile there he was a member of the Journal's editorial board from 1995 to 2001. He wrote a weekly column; "*On the trail*," for the Journal's opinion page from 2000 to 2011 and also contributed to the Journal's newsletter *Political Diary*. Some of his columns have been published in *Esquire*, *Readers Digest*, *Reason*, *The New Republic*, and *National Review*, and others. He has co-written the book *Cleaning House*, with James Coyne. Fund has also collaborated with Rush Limbaugh on a 1992 book *America's Campaign for Term Limits* (ISBN 0-89526-516-8) *the ways things ought to be* (ISBN 067175145X) transcribing it from tape and editing it. In 2004, Fund wrote *Stealing Elections*: How voter fraud threatens our Democracy (ISBN 1-59403-061-8), in which he strongly criticizes the American election system, describing it as "befitting an Emerging Third Worlds country rather than the world's leading democracy." He published an updated edition of the book in 2008 (ISBN 1-59403-224-6). In 2012, Fund and Hans von Spakovsky wrote *who's Country?* How Fraudsters and Bureaucrats Put Your Vote at Risk, in these writings he argues voter fraud is a significant issue in US elections. In his early days, he received the Warren Brookes Award for journalistic excellence from the American Legislative Exchange Council. He also wrote *who is Kyrsten Sinema? It's complicated!* She certainly is; people have followed her all over the country, in airplanes, and bathrooms, she has not been an easy target. Fund has also focused on Manchin, with regards to the voter-ID issues. During his tenure on the Wall Street Journal editorial board, Hawaii State Senator Sam Slom invited John Fund to Honolulu to speak at a luncheon of Small Business Hawaii. I was a member of that organization and had the opportunity to meet him there, but all we did was chat and shake hands, long before the Covet fiasco was an issue. He is the author of several books. Sydney Blumenthal seems to not have liked some of Fund's comments. Roll Call, newspaper of Capitol Hill, called him the "Tom Paine of the modern Congressional reform movement." (not sure what he meant by that), He has awards from the Institute for Justice, The School choice alliance and the Warren Brooks Award for journalistic excellence fro the American Legislative Exchange Council.

Rosemary Jensen (453)

Annie Jensen grew up in Africa and has visited almost every country there and been intimately familiar with Rafiki (*meaning friend*). She has authored several books; along with her husband Dr Robert Jensen are the founders of *Rafiki Foundation*. Since 1997 she saw a great expansion of serious medical deficiencies in Kenya, Uganda, Nigeria, and Ghana as well as other areas of Africa, an increasing number of doctors, dentists, teachers and Christian business people answered God's call to bring medical assistance and Bible teaching to the African people. The secular world assumed that if Planned Parenthood would flood the continent with condoms, its founder Margaret Sanger stated; "*We do not want the word to go out that we want to exterminate the Negro population*," that philosophy might solve the AIDS issue which has overwhelmed the African continent with the needs of millions of orphans due to the epidemic. In response to this crisis Rosemary Jensen decided to help in providing physical, spiritual, and educational, needs for these orphans and vulnerable children of Africa, as well as adults, and organized Rafiki Training Villages in ten of the poorest countries of sub-Saharan Africa. Dr Robert Jensen died in 2014, but that did not end their ministry. In 2009, Rafiki began to publish and distribute its school curriculum including the Rafiki Bible Study to African church schools. In countries where educational materials are in short supply, the curriculum is a tremendous gift and is another tangible way that is befriending these African children. In 2015 the capstone of this came to fruition. The Rafiki Institute of Classical Education (RICE) is a Teachers College to equip educators, in math, science, history, philosophy, theology and many more; graduates are integrated into local church schools across Africa. When they returned to the United States Rosemary was appointed executive director of Bible Study Fellowship, (BSF), an International in-depth Bible Study that meets every week in more than a thousand classes in many countries, and served in that capacity twenty years. She has been president of the Rafiki Foundation for twenty-five years. Why did she write Christian books? It was to know God and spent my quiet time each morning going through the Bible and organized thirty-one attributes of God, one for each day of the month. This took me four years and has influenced my life more than anything else I have ever done. Just this year Ligonier Ministries, and Rafiki, are committed to send 100,000 Reformation Study Bibles, to those in leadership training, giving them more than just a Bible, the Reformation Study Bible contains a series of commentaries by Biblical scholars, such as 75 pastors and theologians around the world, including maps, concordance tables, and historical creeds, given to serious Bible students preparing for ministry.

James H. Case (454)

James H. Case was born April 10, 1920 on Steam Plow Alley, Grove Farm Plantation, Lihue Kauai on a sugar plantation in the Territory of Hawaii, about 40 years before Hawaii became the 50th State; he went to elementary school in Lihue, Kauai, there were 120 students in the class divided in four sections of 30 students each; Jim was the only Caucasian boy in his class with two Caucasian girls. Most of the children spoke Japanese at home therefore many needed special training in English. Jim learned good English, but on the playground spoke pidgin. He got a scholarship and was able to go to Punahou School where 25% of the coed student body were from neighbor Islands or rural Oahu and boarded at school. He graduated as Valedictorian in 1937 and got a scholarship to Williams College in Massachusetts, after graduating, he applied for officer training school but due to being near-sighted he was declined. He went on to Harvard Law School and concentrated on corporate law and taxes. During his 2nd year he met Suzi who later became his wife they were married September 18, 1948 and settled in Hawaii. He went to Mr. Carlsmith in Hilo for a position, and told him, my wife has to finish college and we have to get a job in Honolulu. I was sure that you could help me. He did not offer him a job but did so later and on November 1 1951 he started work at Carlsmith and Cox in Hilo thereby spanning a career over six decades to his retirement in 2012 at age 92. Sixty-one of those years were with Hawaii's oldest law firm Carlsmith Ball, founded in Hilo, Kingdom of Hawaii in 1857. The firm grew from three Hilo lawyers into one of the largest and most prominent law firms in the Pacific and has a legacy deep in Hawaii's history. Their clients and lawyers have left their footprints on the Hawaii culture. He wrote the book "_Hawaii Lawyer_" (Lessons in law from a six-decade career). Reading his book of 299 pages cover to cover, I discovered many of my friends and clients in there. I spend four decades in my financial career and found his book very intriguing and discovered a lot about things. I did not know. To the best of my knowledge, I have never met Jim Case, but it is possible that we crossed paths at business luncheons at such places as Rotary lunch meetings or other public venues. For years I knew of him and may have crossed paths at various business meetings. In his book he writes about many issues not commonly known to me. He writes about the first Waihine (lady) in the legal profession in 1888. He explains the post-war years all the way through to Statehood in 1959. His stories in the book offer insights into continuing a productive and meaningful career deep into one's senior years. It's a refreshing insight and perspective from one of the finest legal minds in the islands from a direction I had never seen; I learned a lot.

Jimmy Stewart (455)

James Maitland Stewart, known to us as Jimmy Stewart was born in Indiana Pennsylvania on May 20, 1908; eldest child and only son of Elizabeth and Alexander Maitland Stewart; He attended Indiana normal school, and Mercersburg Academy, and Princeton University. The family hoped Jimmy would work at the hardware store and thought eventually he would do that. He graduated from Princeton with a degree in Architecture, and due to the depression, there were no jobs available, he helped prepare for a Broadway show in New York. He liked it and followed suit. First, he got small parts and those led to leading roles until he was discovered by Hollywood. In 1935 he signed a contract with MGM studios and began his impressive film career. During the 1930's he made 21 feature films and continued to hone his acting skills. He stared in films with Spencer Tracy, Ginger Rogers, Marlene Dietrich, Clark Gable, Jean Harlow, and many other big names in Hollywood movies; MGM cast him in musicals, drama, comedies, and westerns and won the New York critics award. He starred with Cary Grant and Katherine Hepburn. In the 1940's Jimmy Stewart was riding high and MGM was expecting big results. But he surprised them all, and decided to follow the tradition of his family and enlisted in the military to the dismay of MGM. His third great grandfather served in the Revolutionary War; his maternal grandfather was a general for the Union in the Civil War. His father Alex served in both the Spanish-American War and WW-I. Jimmy entered the Army as a private and at the end of WW-II was a colonel in the Army Air Corps, fully decorated as the result of his bombing missions he flew over Germany as leader of a squadron of B-24 Heavy bombers. Jimmy was awarded two distinguished flying crosses and other awards. He did not say: I completed my obligation and want out, NO! He continued his military career serving in the Air Force Reserves and rose to the rank of Brigadier General; President Reagan awarded him the Medal of Freedom. Top military leaders thought Jimmy should not go to the front but he would not have it and flew 20 combat missions. Following the war, Jimmy went right back to the business of making movies. During the 1950's he collaborated with some of the greatest directors of his time such as Alfred Hitchcock, Billy Wilder, John Ford and others. During the mid 1950's Jimmy Stewart was the top male at the box office for many years. In 1949 he married Gloria Hatrick McLean, they had twin daughters, and Jimmy settled down to family life. On July 2, 1997 Jimmy Stewart died at age 89 in Beverly Hills and left this legacy, quoting his co-workers: "_He was as likable in real life as he was on the screen._" When Alfred Hitchcock was asked, he said "Imagine anyone hating Jimmy Stewart?"

Audrey Hepburn (456)

Audrey Kathleen Ruston was born 4 May, 1929 in Ixelles, Brussels, and spent her childhood in Belgium, England and the Netherlands, she was known to her family as Adriaantje. He mother Baroness Ella van Heemstra was a Dutch Noblewoman; her father Joseph Victor Anthony Ruston, was a British subject born in Auschitz, Bohemia Austria-Hungary, he was an Honorary British Consul in the Dutch East Indies. Hepburn's parents were married in Batavia Dutch East Indies (now Indonesia) in 1926, later moved to London, and on to Brussels; they lived in The Hague, Arnhem and London. As a result of her multinational background, she learned six languages, Dutch and English, French, German, Spanish and Italian; (like most of us who grew up in the European multi lingual environment, we are not experts, but can converse in multi languages). In the mid 1930's she had a serious fall out with her father who left abruptly; mentioning later of being "dumped." And said <u>children need two parents.</u> Joseph moved to London and never visited his daughter abroad. She said; <u>it was the most traumatic event of my life</u>." In 1952 she was engaged, fitted for the wedding dress, and called it off, saying: "The demands of her career would keep us apart, I want to be <u>really</u> married". Later Gregory Peck introduced her to Mel Ferrer, and on 25 Sept. 1954 they were married in Switzerland, and had a son called Sean. She claimed it was a good marriage but admitted to her bad temper, resulting in divorce. Then she married Italian psychiatrist Andrea Dotti, in 1969 and had a son Luca Andrea. The American Film Institute named her among the greatest Female stars of all time, staring in a number of successful films winning Golden Globe, Oscar, and Tony Awards; starred in Sabrina, Funny Face, My Fair Lady, with lead performers such as Humphrey Bogart, Gregory Peck, Cary Grant, and many more. One of the primary reasons she is on this page; she put her career on hold in WW-II and was active in the resistance movement, risked her life, experienced hunger, rescued Jews, sheltered Allied soldiers, was arrested by the Gestapo, but escaped. She was invited to play a role in the film, "<u>The Diary of Anne Frank</u>", but that was too close to home and turned it down, she met Anne's father, Holocaust survivor <u>Otto Frank</u>. She also declined a role in the movie "<u>A Bridge too far</u>". (I understand her not wanting to re-live those years.) When she was too sick to travel, a longtime friend arranged for a private jet, filled with flowers to fly her from California to Switzerland, and on 20 January 1993, Audrey Hepburn died in her sleep and was interred in a Swiss Cemetery amid flower arrangements from Gregory Peck, Elizabeth Taylor and the Dutch Royal Family. She left us a legacy that endured for years in movie theaters around the world as well as in many people's memories.

David Niven (457)

James David Graham Niven was born 1 March 1910 in London England; he attended Heatherdown Preparatory School and Stowe School and the Royal Military College Sandhurst. Then he joined the British Army and was commissioned a second lieutenant in the Highlands Light Infantry. His father William Niven was of Scottish descent, his grandfather was from St Martin's Village in Perthshire. Lieutenant William Niven was killed in the First World War in Gallipoli in August 1915. His mother Henriette was born in Wales; her father was Major William Degacher of the 1st Battalion, 24th Regiment of Foot, was killed at the battle of Isandlwana in the Anglo-Zulu War in 1879. Later his mother re-married Conservative politician Sir Thomas Comyn Platt, sold their London home and moved to the Isle of Wight; in his 1971 biography, Niven wrote fondly of his childhood home, his stepfather put him in boarding school. There he described bullying and abuse; the older boys would often assault younger boys; the school masters were the same; one sadistic teacher would pull my ears half way out of his head. Growing up he was interested in acting first as an extra. He started in the British film _there goes the Bride_ (1932). Bored with the peacetime army, he resigned his commission in 1933, relocated to New York, on to Hollywood, hired an agent and got small parts in films; including a non-speaking roll in Mutiny on the Bounty, that brought him to wider attention in the film industry; got hired for parts in major motion pictures such as: the Light Brigade (1936), the Prisoner of Zenda (1937), by 1938 he was starring as the leading man in 'A' films. In World War-II, he returned to Britain and rejoined the army as a lieutenant. In 1942 he co-starred in the morale-building film about the development of the Supermarine Spitfire fighter, _the first of the few_ (American title Spitfire), which was enthusiastically endorsed by Winston Churchill. After the war he resumed his acting career and was voted 2nd most popular British actor in a Popularity Poll. He appeared in _a matter of Life and Death_ (1946), _The Bishop's Wife_ (1947) with Cary Grant, _The Toast of New Orleans_ (1950), _Happy Go Lovely_ (1951_), Happy ever after_ (1954), _Around the World in 80 days_ (1956), He acted in more than 100 films, and did many shows for television, and wrote at least four books with considerable commercial success. He divided his time between Switzerland and France. Those who were close to him, said he never ever lost his temper, his countenance was of elegance with much humor, and he was all class. In 1983 (using a false name to avoid publicity) he was hospitalized for 10 days, checked out and returned to his Chalet at Chateau-d' (Ex. His condition worsened and he died at age 73 at home on 29 July 1983 and was buried with an attendance of 1200 in the local cemetery in Switzerland.

Paul Newman (458)

Paul Leonard Newman was born 26 January 1925 in the affluent community of Shaker Heights, suburb of Cleland Ohio. He is the 2nd son of Arthur Sigmund Newman and Theresa Fetsko. A Jewish business family migrated from Poland and Hungary and owned a successful sporting goods store. At age 25 Paul was kicked out of Ohio University where he belonged to the Phi Kappa Tau Fraternity, for unruly behavior. He served three years in the United States Navy during World War II as a radio operator, graduated from Ohio's Kenyon College, and married Jacqueline "Jackie" Witte; in that same year his father died. When he became successful in later years, he said he regretted that his father was not around to see his son's success. While doing a play at Yale University he was spotted by two agents who invited him to New York City to pursue a professional acting career. In New York he got a few guest spots; in 1953 came a big break, he got a lead role in the successful Broadway play "_Picnic_" and while doing that he met actress Joanne Woodward who was in the play. There was a strong attraction, got on so well, they were married in 1958 in Las Vegas. Newman never auditioned but was accepted into the much admired and popular New York Actors Studio. In 1954, a film Newman had been reluctant to do, was released, _The Silver Chalice_ (1954). He considered his performance epic to be so bad that he took out a full-page ad in a trade paper apologizing for it to anyone who might have seen it. He had always been embarrassed about the film and reveled in making fun of it. He immediately wanted to return to the stage and performed in "_The desperate hours_" in 1956, he got a chance to redeem himself in the film world by portraying Rocky Graziano in "_Somebody up there likes me_ (1956) and critics praised the performance. In 1957 with a handful of films to his credit he was cast in _The Long Hot Summer_ (1958) Co starring Joanne Woodward. In 1969 Paul Newman and Robert Redford Acted together for the first time in _Butch Cassidy and the Sundance kid_ (1969) it was a box office smash. Films were not the only thing on his mind, Paul was a passionate race car driver and was co-founder of Newman-Haas racing, they owned their own car, and in 26 years the team won 107 races and 8 championships. Paul also founded Newman's Own, a successful line of food products that has earned in excess of $100-million, and donated every penny to charity. He was known for his many philanthropic ways and highly successful business ventures and was very proud to find himself on President Nixon's enemy list. His marriage to Woodward lasted a half century. Paul Newman was a smoker for many years and died from lung cancer at age 83 on September 26, 2008 in Westport Connecticut. Joan Woodward outlives him but suffers from Alzheimer and requires 24/7 care.

Clark Gable (459)

William Clark Gable was born on February 1, 1901 in Cadiz, Ohio, to Adeline (Hershelman) and William Henry Gable, an oil-well driller. He was of German, Irish, and Swiss-German descent. When he was six moths old his mother had him baptized as a Roman Catholic, but then at the next month, (he was still a baby at seven months), his mother died. His father needed to work and Gable was sent to live with his maternal aunt and uncle in Pennsylvania, where he stayed until he was two, then went back to his father. At age 16 he quit high school to work in a tire factory in Akron Ohio. After seeing a play, *The Bird of Paradise*, he decided to become an actor. On December 13, 1924, he married Josephine Dillon, (his acting coach 15 years his senior). They moved to Hollywood and got divorced a year later. He then married Maria Langham; 17 years older than him. He was where he wanted to be and began his acting career working as an extra. The first film where he had a roll was in *The Painted Desert* (1931). It did not take long to get noticed in the film industry and soon his acting career did so well, he was compelled to refuse work. Gable starred in *Call of the wild* (1935), *Mutiny on the Bounty* (1935), *Wife vs. Secretary* (1936), San *Francisco* (1936), *Too Hot to Handle* (1938) *Gone with the wind* (1939), In 1939 he married Carol Lombard, but in 1942 she died in a plane crash, he was grief stricken, and America was embroiled in World War II, on two fronts. Gable put his career aside and joined the US Army Air Force and was off the screen for three years. Instead, he flew combat missions in Europe. When the war ended, he did not renew his contract and freelanced. But that did not go to well and his films did not attract an audience at the box office. On November 16, 1959 he became a grandfather when Judy Lewis his daughter gave birth to baby Maria. He was a good actor, often referred to as "The King of Hollywood". His golden days were before my time and in the 1930's Gable firmly cemented his status as a cinematic legend he starred in the now classic romantic comedy film *It happened one night*, (1934). People saw him at the peak of his acting ability and his popular appeal, as he often portrayed a down to earth bravado character with a carefree attitude. He was known as the epitome of masculinity with his unmatched charm and knowing smile, and was named the seventh greatest male star of classic American cinema by the American Film Institute. He had roles in more than sixty motion pictures during a career that lasted 37 years. In November1960 he had just completed filming the Misfits (1961) when he suffered a heart attack, and died at age 59 later that month, and was buried at Forest Lawn Memorial Park at Glendale.

Sissel Kyrkjebo (460)

It was 1994 and our family was ready to watch TV and see the Lillehammer winter sports in Norway; it opened with that majestic Olympic Hymn sung by one of my favorite European classical crossover sopranos 25-year-old Sissel Kyrkjebo with the children's chorus singing: "*Ancient flame immortal, whose beacon lights our way*," as composed by Greek Composer Spyridan Samara performed for the first time at the 1896 summer Olympics in Athens. Sissel was magnificent; I immediately called my friend Audun in Larvik Norway and told him she had become my favorite European performer. He responded: "On your next Swiss meeting stop by Norway and meet her she is a family friend; since then, I have stopped many times but never made it to Oslo. Sissel was born 24 June, 1969 in Bergen, (meaning Mountains). She is considered one of the world's top crossover sopranos. Her musical style ranges from pop recordings and folk songs to classical vocals and operatic arias. Sissel has a "crystalline" voice and wide vocal range, sings mainly in English and Norwegian, but has also sung in Swedish, Danish, Irish, Italian, French, Russian, Icelandic, German, Latin, Maori, and Japanese. She became known around the world for singing the Olympic hymn at the opening and closing ceremonies of the 1994 Winter Olympics in Norway; and the Christmas in Vienna concert of 1994; as well as her participation on the Titanic film soundtrack. She received her first US Grammy nomination in December 2007 for collaboration with the Mormon Tabernacle Choir, and was nominated for the best classical crossover album of the year as well as Best Engineered Classical Album. Sissel's combined solo record sales (not including soundtracks and other albums to which she contributed), amount to 10 million albums sold, mostly in Norway, a country with 5 million people, as well as in Sweden, Denmark and Japan. She is one of the few Norwegian artists to have an album go 11 times platinum in album sales. Her first name is the Norwegian variant of Cecilia. She grew up with two older brothers, Erik and Bjorn. The family often took hikes in the surrounding mountains around Bergen. She originally wanted to be a nurse, but at age nine, music became her passion and joined her first children's choir under the direction of New Zealand born conductor Felicity Laurence and took seven years of musical education. They sang classical, jazz, folk, and Maori songs. Because they had this very clean pure sound, people said it sounded like an angel choir. She won her first local talent competition at age ten. Her first solo appearance was in 1984 when she sang the Norwegian folk tune Ung Aslaug. Despite being world famous, now being a superstar, she has kept her life as normal as possible, *that* earned her a page here.

Shirley Temple (461)

Shirley Jane Temple was born April 23, 1928, in Santa Monica California. At a dance school she was spotted by Charles Lamont who was a casting director for Educational Pictures; he took a liking to her and invited her for an audition. She did, along with several other children, but Temple became the breakout star and was promoted for a roll in a series of 20-minute comedies; with no further competition Shirley began her film career at age three in 1931. Two years later she received international fame in feature film *Bright Eyes*. She received a special Juvenile Academy Award in 1935 for her outstanding talent and performance for such motion pictures as *Curly Top*, and *Heidi*, the movie producers capitalized on her wholesome image, and received numerous awards as a child-star. When the parents were celebrating her successes over a special dinner, in a classy restaurant with some of their favorite wine, the waiter mixed up a special non-alcoholic drink served in a fancy child glass for her, so she could feel special too; however, all good things come to an end and her box-office popularity waned as she reached adolescence. She appeared in 29 films from age 3 to 10, but only in 14 films from age 14 to 21. In 1950 at age 22 Shirley retired from filming. In 1958 Temple returned to show business with two season television anthology series of fairy tale adaptations. She made guest appearances on television shows in the early 1960's and filmed a sitcom pilot that was never released. She sat on the boards of corporations and organizations including The Walt Disney Company, Del Monte Foods and the National Wildlife Federation. She began a diplomatic career when President Richard Nixon appointed her to Represent America to the United Nations, and later served as 9th US Ambassador to Ghana serving there from 1974 to 1976, after that was US Ambassador to Czechoslovakia from 1989 to 1992. At age 44 in 1972 Shirley was diagnosed with breast cancer. The tumor was removed and a modified radical mastectomy performed. At that time such items were typically discussed in hushed whispers, but Shirley announced the disease, and her operation on radio and television, and in a February 1973 article for the Magazine McCall's. Shirley Temple rose to stardom as a child in the 1930s in a world that was suffering from the Great Depression and dealing with the rising tensions of World War II; an adorable child smiling, singing and dancing. Indefatigable positive, watching scenes of her old movies, it's impossible to miss the broad smiles which are clearly something more than just acting for a generation troubled by war and poverty. That little girl represented hope for the future. She survived the breast cancer and died from Pneumonia and Chronic Obstructive Pulmonary Disease (COPD) at age 85 on February 10, 2014; we miss the little princess.

Albert L Ireland (462)

Albert Luke Ireland was born February 25, 1918 in Cold Spring Nelsonville, New York, He was a lifetime member of the Cold Spring Fire Department; According to his bio he served in 1941 in the Royal Canadian Air Force, no further details are given what he did, nor why he enlisted in the RCAF at the very beginning of World War II, (I lived in Europe at that time and can not explain how Americans living in the US can serve in a foreign country in military service, and do not understand the 1896 US Supreme Court ruling on that issue.) Having said that; later 1941 Ireland enlisted in the US Marine Corps and served 27 months overseas in World War II as a machine gunner and was wounded in the Guadalcanal Campaign, it did not stop him; he fought in the Battle of Okinawa and was wounded four more times. After the war he served in the Marine Corps Reserve, took classes in Health and Education at Ithaca College between 1948 and 1949, to the University of Arizona and the University of Notre Dame. He was called back to Active duty in the fall of 1950 after the outbreak of the Korean War. He completed a refresher combat training at Camp Lejeune, and in early January 1951 he applied for combat duty, but a first sergeant who was creating the list of Marines to be sent to Korea, attempted to prevent him from going. He already got two purple hearts, and according to Marine Corps regulations he should not go back to a war zone. Ireland appealed that ruling to General Clifton B. Cates in Washington DC the Commandant of the Marine Corps. The outcome was: Ireland was flown from Washington to Korea, and went back to war exactly what he wanted to do. In Korea went to the front lines and was wounded in the leg, hand, neck and face. In 1953 Sergeant Albert Ireland was honorably discharged from the Marine Corps. The reason he is on these pages, is because he is the recipient of nine purple hearts, the most (or second most), ever awarded to a single individual since its inception after April 1917 (perhaps Curry Thomas Haynes exceeded that with one more). Ireland was awarded five for actions in World War II while serving in the Pacific theatre, four more during the Korea conflict, and earned eight battle stars, a bronze star and two other citations. He proved his commitment to the Fatherland with having received nine purple hearts. He died at age 79 on November 16, 1997; a section of New York State Route 301 was named after Ireland, and for his dedication of faithful service to his country as well as the years he was a member of the Cold Spring fire department. Albert L. Ireland died in Kansas; his remains were taken for burial in Cold Spring NY. The Sheriff's department there named a <u>Marine Patrol Boat</u> after Ireland; it currently patrols the Hudson River.

Kay Coles James (463)

Madeline Kay Coles was born on June 1, 1949 in Portsmouth Virginia US Her mother was on government welfare for some of her youth. She was raised in the inner city of Richmond Virginia, and was the only girl out of 5 boys. Her father left home when she was four years old, she was raised by an aunt and uncle both professional people. He was a businessman and she was a school teacher, although there was an alcohol issue in that home. Kay attended John Marshall High School and Hampton University receiving numerous honorary degrees including a Doctor of Laws from Pepperdine University. She served at Fairfax County School Board and the Virginia Board of Education, and was on the board of Focus on the Family, and was Senior Vice President of Family Research Council in Washington DC. She was appointed by President Ronald Reagan and re-appointed by President George H.W, Bush as member of the National Commission on Children. She served as Associate Director of the White House Office of National Drug Control Policy and as Assistant Secretary of Public Affairs at the US Department of Health and Human Services. She was Convention Secretary for the Republican National Convention, when Bob Dole was nominated for President. Kay served as the director for the United States Office of Personnel Management in the George W. Bush administration. On Dec.19, 2017 the Heritage Foundation announced that Kay Coles would be their sixth president. She had served as a member of the Board of Trustees since 2005, and was the first black person and the first female to serve in that position. Heritage Foundation is a conservative American think tank based in Washington DC, founded on February 16, 1973 by Paul Weyrich, Edwin Feulner, and Joseph Coors, advocating for pro-business policies, anti-communism and neo-conservatism and the Christian right of the 1970's. In early 1980 they published a mandate for Leadership, focusing on reducing the size of government. President Reagan liked that mandate and gave a copy to each member of his cabinet; since than the foundation has taken a leading role and continued to influence conservative policies in the United States, she told the Atlantic. In a newspaper interview Kay said: "I came from, what you call a dysfunctional family." I never met Kay, but have been associated with the Heritage Foundation since my friend Paul Weyrich organized it in 1973, and we are very proud to have someone with her leadership qualities as our new leader; Time magazine called Heritage "the foremost of the new breed advocacy tanks," Kay is mother to three grown children and the wife of Charles James who was Deputy Assistant Secretary of the office of Federal Contract Compliance Program appointed by President George W. Bush.

Michele Bachmann (464)

Michele Marie Bachmann Amble was born April 6, 1956 in Waterloo Iowa to her Norwegian American family, and grew up in a Democrat home; She was raised in the Norwegian Lutheran church, but has withdrawn their membership and changed it to the Evangelical Free Church of America. She has cited the influence from people such as theologian Francis Schaeffer. Politically she changed to Republican during her senior year at Winona State University in 1987 after reading the book *Christianity and the Constitution* which argues that the United States was founded as a Christian theocracy and should become one again. In 1986 Bachman received a J.D. degree from Oral Roberts University. She was a member of the ORU law school's final graduating class, and was part of a group, faculty, staff, and students, who moved the law library to Regent University. She left the IRS to become a full-time mother when her fourth child was born. As a Democrat she watched Francis Schaeffer's 1976 documentary *How shall we then live?* And was supportive of the anti abortion sidewalk interference. At first, she supported Jimmy Carter for president, but became disappointed with his liberal approach favoring legalized abortion and misguided economic decisions, resulting in high gas prices. In 1980 she voted for Ronald Reagan and began working for his presidential election. She formally entered politics in 2000 and began to speak out strongly against legalized abortion. In 1993 along with other parents they started the K-12 New Heights Charter School in Stillwater. The publicly funded school's charter mandated that it be non-sectarian in all programs and practices, but the school soon developed a strong Christian orientation, and people complained. This propelled Michele into politics in 2000 she was elected to the Minnesota State Senate, and in 2006 was elected to the US House of Representatives, and re-elected for a second term. When in office she visited Pakistan, Kuwait, and Iraq and others. In Pakistan they had to travel in armored vehicles and were constantly accompanied by Pakistani military. We were able to see up close what its like to be in a region where fighting is occurring; and saw the dangers posed by Islamic terrorism in Iraq. She justified the continuous presence of British and American military there, we don't want to see al-Qaida get a presence in the United States. In 2014 she retired from Congress and together with her husband owns a Christian Counseling practice. Her husband has a Ph.D. degree. They have been foster parents to 23 children most of the being teenage girls, with such issues as eating disorders who were patients at the University of Minnesota program; their home was legally defined as a treatment home.

Lowell Smith Dillingham (465)

Lowell Smith Dillingham was born June 17, 1911 in the family home at the corner of Punahou and Beretania Street, (now Central Union Church) in Honolulu. There were no fences dividing homes, he recalls a happy childhood; growing up in that environment waiting about two blocks from home for his father to come by in his new chandler, then climb in and ride home with daddy. His first school was Lanai-school on Kewalo Street Miss Maxwell was the head mistress. At one time the area was a cow pasture. His mother wanted him in an Eastern boarding school but had some difficulty getting a place for him. He went to Harvard where he had four glorious years but did not graduate, right after he went to work at Hawaiian dredging. His early job was at Pearl Harbor after the December 1941 bombing damage, the company was asked to move the moorings so the _Tennessee_ could be pulled out, they worked day and night removing these moorings, using much dynamite, next the _West Virginia_; while doing that, the Navy asked them to build a runway on Johnson Island he said: "Where is Johnson Island?" The Navy brought a map showing that it was about 1,000 miles south. While Japan was bombing Pearl Harbor a Japanese submarine had fired on Johnson Island, and there were only a few guns and a few hundred marines. Lowell went there for six months and his company built a runway so that fighter planes from Kaneohe could fly and land there. Japan had also attacked Kwajelein, his company was busy during, and after, World War II, doing clean up and build harbors and air strip throughout the Pacific and did three jobs in the Suez Canal. Lowell Dillingham flew around the world three times a year. Next, he began building Ala Moana shopping center in the 50-acre parcel; he needed to attract a few anchor retailers and negotiated with McInerny, Sears, Liberty House, Nordstrom, Macy, as well as the Hawaii Visitors Bureau, the University, Landscape contractors, Architects etc. He did that, and Hawaii got Ala Moana Center. He owned a home in a luxury condo complex at Diamondhead which I insured during my business days. I was always invited and attended many board meetings. It was there that I met Lowell on many occasions and greatly appreciated his wisdom during these meetings. I learned a lot from him, and had many opportunities to stay after and chat with him there. He was very business savvy I enjoyed chatting with him; in 1969 he became chief Executive officer and president of the company. During the 1970's I told him that his business expertise could be valuable at the Hawaii State Legislature where I often lobbied. I can not print his response here. However, he changed his mind and did serve in 1984. In total he made great contributions to Hawaii. Lowell Dillingham died at Queens medical center at age 76 on August 14, 1987 in Honolulu.

Sendor Nemeth (466)

Sendor Nemeth is the pastor of Faith Church that was founded in 1979 by a group of 7 Hungarian believers in Budapest Hungary. It is an Independent Pentecostal-Charismatic-church, which in 2008 had 30,000 people worshipping there and in 2016 about 70,000 believers attend weekly worship services, their services are broadcast on life television. From 1945 to 1989 Hungary was ruled by communist dictators, meaning the activities of pastor Nemeth were monitored by the Communist secret service, thereby creating a hunger for the Gospel, What the Communist dictators not seem to know is that persecution is the seed of the church, and instead of killing the church it has the opposite affect. Opposition and conflict between the world and the church has existed more than 2,000 years but even before that, in early days of the Old Testament, 66 people went in to Egypt and 430 years later Moses led 20,000 to 2 million out of Egypt. (Scholars disagree over these numbers, and I was not there, so we will leave it at that. We do know the people grew under persecution of the Egyptian rulers.) The change in education has experienced many changes in Hungary; the level of youngsters has been growing year by year. Students attending Bornemisza High School or other schools have been able to debate theological issues with Catholics and have a wide knowledge of theology, the Bible, God, and the story of man. Not only can these young people sensibly discuss and defend what they belief and explain why they believe. There is still confusion in the educational system of the Hungarian Schools especially when it relates to Job preparation. This is of great importance to these large mega churches. It is very important to have a solid teaching Bible school. A mega church like that brings many responsibilities especially in Eastern Europe, Pastor Nemeth is greatly concerned that his people can be a witness for their faith in Eastern Europe and have a sound worldview when they step into the adult world. He would like his youth to study Medicine, Philosophy, Political Science, and remain strong in their faith in their secular society. When Daniel was a success in a foreign land, he still prayed three times a day because he needed that, but it landed him in the den of lions. In Hungary persecution has not been foreign. In his struggles to find answers he consulted with another Mega Church pastor and visited David Yonggi Cho in Korea, also a Pentecostal Church who attracts 480,000 worshippers on weekends. I have watched the Resurrection Sunday dance of Faith Church in Budapest square for many years, it is beautiful to see these thousands of young people after having for many of their growing up years been subjected to Communism, now filling that huge Budapest square with singing and dancing, thanks to the vision God gave to pastor Sendor Nemeth.

David Yonggi Cho (467)

David Yonggi Cho was born February 14, 1936 in the rural county of Ulju in South Korea, his father went bankrupt. At his age 17, tuberculosis sent him to a hospital, he was coughing up blood and began re-thinking his Buddhist worldview that taught he must suffer; he cried out to God and said "I want to live, please help me." He was miraculously cured and gave glory to God and went to Full Gospel Bible College. After graduating in 1958; (with his future mother-in-law Jashil Choi), they started *Yoido Full Gospel Church* in Seoul Korea, began worship services in a tent pieced together from US Army tents, affiliated the church with the Assemblies of God and attracted about 5 or 6 people at the first service. (As a teenager he had learned some English while hanging around American military basis). The two pastors began a vigorous campaign of knocking on doors, helping the poor, pray for the sick and in a few months had 50 people, before long 600; when it reached 2400 it plateaued for several years. He then developed the idea of cell groups and empowered 20 deaconesses to develop groups in twenty districts in the city, and refined these groups in to leadership training, and by 1973 the church had about 18,000 members and built a new building in Yoido, which is the financial district of Seoul. They kept growing eventually in to the largest church in the world with seven weekly services claiming a membership of 830,000 worshippers. Some time ago I attended a seminar in Los Angeles and listened to 3 speakers explaining what is involved in a mega church and it made my head spin, although none of them had reached the level of pastor Cho. What goes in to the organization of a church that is that size? A pastor becomes the CEO of a large corporation. Just filling the pulpit with the right speakers, one person can not do this, it takes a team, of like minded and capable associates, train and supervise all the cell group leaders with the right teaching material, know the church's teaching philosophy, caring for the poor, music people, visiting the sick and elderly, conduct funerals, education material for kindergarten through college, Bible College and Seminary. Social issues such as abortion, drugs, Homosexuality capable teachers, leaders, ushers, Parking, Traffic directors for many blocks, Police, Fire and emergencies, teachers for small groups, youth leaders, what about foreign languages who will control teaching material and hundreds more. Pastor Cho retired from ministry in 2008 and on 14 September 2021 he died at National University Hospital in Seoul of complication from a stroke. Many issues during his ministry have surfaced such as ancestor worship, misappropriations of funds, and many more; we have no information about these investigations and outcome. Pastor Cho made a major difference big time he was a simple sinner, saved by grace.

David Warren (468)

David Warren was born 20 March 1925 on Groote Eylandt, (_big Island_), a small Island a few miles of the northern coast of Australia. At age four he was sent to Tasmania and Sydney to spend the next 12 years in boarding schools, When David was 9 years old in 1934, Australia experienced the first major Air Crash that claimed the life of his father. Twenty years later the age of commercial jet aircraft was just beginning, and he worked as a research chemist at the aeronautical research laboratories in Melbourne investigating the mysterious 1953 crash of a Comet jetliner. While people argued about the possible cause, he reasoned, if someone had a Protona Minifon Recorder that he saw at a trade fair, it was fire proof, and erase itself saving the last hours. The device consisted of a single steel wire and provided four hours of recording medium. The item was well received in England where the idea of the _Black Box_ was made up by journalist at a briefing and also in Canada where it was seen as a potential addition to beacons being developed. He continued to lead the project, developing the flight memory devise to record more instruments with greater accuracy. This led to the first commercially produced flight recorder – The Red Egg. A further disaster at Wintoon in 1967 saw Australia become the first country to make both fight data and cockpit voice mandatory in all jets. The recorder, (_the black box_), is installed in the most crash survivable part of an aircraft, usually the tail section. The data collected in that black box can help investigators determine whether an accident was caused by pilot error, by an external event such a windshear, or by an airplane system problem. The flight data recorder is virtually indestructible. The recovered flight recorder may not have saved lives in _that_ flight, but if recovered and determined the cause, it may resemble the light house, we never know how many lives it has saved. Wile David was at the University of Sydney, he met Ruth Meadows who became his wife and lifetime supporter. Together they raised a family and shared an interest in science and education. When he retired, David and Ruth lived in Caulfield South Victoria, which is a community about 12 km South-East of Melbourne, there they could stay in contact with their four children and seven grandchildren. David Warren lived to age 85 and died on 19 July in 2010. He was placed in a casket bearing the label "Flight recorder inventor, do not open". He was a great scientist and in June 2012 the government named a road: David Warren Road in the suburb of Hume in recognition of his great and life saving contribution to science. On 25 March 2014 the Australian Defence Science and Technology Organization, which is located in the Australian capital of Canberra, has renamed their headquarters: the David Warren Building in his honor.

John Gibson Paton (469)

John Gibson Paton was born 24 May 1824 in a farm cottage Braehead, Scotland. He was the eldest of 11 children of James and Janet Paton. From age 12 he worked with his father manufacturing stocking frames fourteen hours a day, and studied during the two hours allotted for meals. During those years he was influenced by his father who would go three times a day to his prayer closet, and conducted family prayers twice a day. Paton felt God called him to serve overseas as a missionary and to prepare for that he went to Glasgow for Medical and Theological studies. On 23 March 1858 he was ordained in the Reformed Presbyterian Church, and on April 2, 1858 he sailed for the South Pacific to be a missionary in New Hebrides. He writes that his father walked them to the ship, embraced each other in tears and parted with prayer. I remember waiving to my father standing there, head uncovered. I looked back and watched through blinding tears where I had left him gazing at me till we were out of site. The elders of the church were seeking somewhat vainly for volunteers to join the family in that hazardous undertaking. When he landed in Tanna, the natives had been entirely untouched by Western civilization, except in so far as they had from time to time been irritated by aggression on the part of sandalwood traders. Upon arrival he discovered natives that were cannibals enveloped in superstitions, cruelty, and of heathenism; certainly, a place where there was a great need for Christianity. He was married to Mary Ann Robson, the young Scotsman and his new wife (without any experience outside the small church to which they belonged), were the first white residents in an island full of naked people, painted wildmen, and cannibals utterly regardless of the value of even their own lives and without any sense of mutual kindness. Beginning his, (humanly speaking), near impossible task; he brought to the natives of the New Hebrides Education and Christianity, while teaching and preaching, he developed small industries for them such as hat-making. His work there was extremely difficult, they took strong position against slavery (called blackbirding), by (New Zealanders and others coming in from outside), kidnapped natives, and forced them to work in slavery. His work was not only difficult but _dangerous._ He tried to educate uncivilized people, preached, raised a family, and worked to get support in Scotland for his missionary work. His wife died; he re-married in 1864, and his new wife Margaret showed strong literary ability and was of great assistance to him. He died at age 82 on 28 January, 1907 and was buried in Boroondara cemetery in Victoria Australia, where he and several children are interred in the same grave. Currently close friends of ours, a young couple with 3 small children serve in Vanuatu, representing Wycliffe Bible Translators.

Michael Gangloff (470)

Michael Gangloff (according to Midweek Nov. 10, 2021), was born in Missouri; his family moved to the islands when he was four, he grew up in Hawaii, and is the man behind all these dazzling Christmas lights displayed at the stadium and at City Hall in Honolulu. The first Christmas was publicly recognized in Hawaii in 1862; and in 1866 King Kamehameha IV and Queen Emma celebrated and observed Thanksgiving and Christmas. Gangloff and his team of volunteers kick off that Christmas-themed extravaganza around mid November every year; especially in this COVID world, it sets a more positive tone. The Aloha Winter Wonderland show at the stadium attracted 45,000 cars, an amazing accomplishment. For many years we took our foster children to the lights at city hall on King Street. According to the article Gangloff is the owner, and CEO of event sponsor MIRA Image construction LLC. He said we live in a negative time, and if we work together and put aside our differences we can come back. I agree and would like to live in UTOPIA, but having been raised under Hitler who made an attempt to change Germany and Europe into a perfect world we all know how that came out. Living in Hawaii Kai may be as close as we get to UTOPIA, specially watching the amazing sunsets. According to Gangloff the beauty of that show will lift the spirits with holiday cheer; he delivers proceeds to several local charities such as Make-a-Wish Hawaii, Kupuna Power, Shriner's Hospital for Children, feed hungry people, create education opportunity for seniors, buy 2.900 turkeys for families in Mayor Wright Homes, Kuhio Park Terrace and deliver the food we save them the waiting lines. He grew up without a biological father; the family was financially strapped and was forced to survive mostly on government assistance. Despite the poverty-stricken circumstances they learned the value of hard work and he credits his stepfather with being a good role model, working four jobs, getting there on a moped. Michael started earning money at age 7 while living in a low rent area in Waipahu. He went door to door and said if I haul your trash away will you give me a penny for each bag. Many would gladly give him that, and let him drag their refuse down the stairs. When he had some coins in his pocket, he would wait for the Manapua wagon. He got 2 bubble gums for 1 cent; 5 cents would buy a soda. In the 80's he hung out at the airport he could get 25 cents returning luggage carts when they reached the check in, he was right there and offered to take the cart. When asked what he would like to change from his childhood? He said "Not one iota." As author of these books, I feel the same, I learned more in my poverty-stricken childhood than all the years later, including school.

Peng Shuai (471)

Peng Shuai was born 8 Jan.1986 in Xianglan, Hunan China. Her father is a police officer. At age 8 she took tennis lessons; At 13 she got heart surgery and began her career in Tennis with Coach Carlos Rodriguez; she can play with right and left hands, very beneficial for a tennis player, she scored high early in her career. In 2001 at age 15 she won her first singles a $10k tournament, and defeating countrywoman Sun Tiantian in the semifinal. In July she won her 2nd ITF tournament of the year. Then in 2003, she put in her career best performance coming through qualifying to win her first $25k title at Jackson Mississippi with match wins against Rika Fijiwara, Tatiana Golovin, and Christina Wheeler, among others. At the end of 2004 her result had pushed her up to No 107 in the rankings gaining entry in the grand slam main draw at Wimbledon but was defeated in straight sets by 14th seed Silvia Farina Elia; that year she ended well. In 2005 she broke her ankle in February, and mist several tournaments; in April she was back but lost two successive 2nd round matches to top ten players Vera Zvonareva and Justine Henin-Hardenne each match running to three close sets. By September 2005 Peng ranked among the top 5 female tennis players across the whole Asian Continent. In 2006 she did not do well in the Australian open; 2007 was slightly better. She was considered one of the world's top players, China was proud of her; At the China open in 2007, Peng beat former <u>No-1</u>- and five-time grand slam champion Martina Hingis in the final match of her career, she also beat Amelie Maurismo en route to her second semifinal of the year. In the autumn Peng suffered a surprising loss in Tier III Guangzhou to Tzipora Obziler and in the qualification tournament for Luxembourg to former top ten player Alicia Molik; she qualified for the main draw of Zurich; Peng finished the year in 2007 with a top ten win against Mauresmo. Being a champion is great, but…. she discovered that to be China's most recognizable sports star, has pros and cons, apparently she posted an incident on social media in 2021; 10 years ago she was invited by the Communist Party Boss to play in Beijing and after, he and his wife asked her for dinner at their home, there she claims was <u>coerced</u> and <u>pressured</u> by him <u>and</u> his wife to have sex with him, kept it to herself for a decade, but in 2021, she posted it on social media that post was deleted almost immediately, and now Peng can not be found. We have admired her for some time and don't think a person of her fame will be invisible for long; China may protect their Communist leaders, but Peng Shuai is a national treasure. China is a master of deception and has successfully advised the country that Tiananmen Square protest was peaceful, but being there in person we know better, will China succeed again?

Harry Weinberg (472)

Harry Weinberg was born August 15, 1908 in Sambor (now Sambir), Austro-Hungarian Empire. After World War I it was annexed to Poland, after World War II it became part of Ukraine. Harry was the second of seven children the parents Joseph and Sarah, both were Jewish, born in 1881; in 1911 the family moved to America and settled in Baltimore Maryland. Harry was ten years old when World War I ended, and never let an opportunity go to waist he took advantage of the spirit of that time and sold small American flags on the street; after sixth grade at the Baltimore public school, he felt he had all the education he needed and helped his father in the body and fender business till he was 18, then emancipated himself and moved to Philadelphia, to work for a tire re-treading company which he later purchased from its owner. In 1928 he moved back to Baltimore; and learned the basic skills about running a retail business. He met Jeanette and in 1931they married. After the great depression that began in late 1929, real Estate and stock prices were relatively low. In 1938 he sponsored several of his wife's relatives to get out of Germany and avoid Nazi persecution to escape the coming genocide of the Jews. In 1941 he tried to enlist in the US Military but had an inoperable hernia and was declared 4F, ineligible, however four family members did serve in the army and the navy; all four returned after the war. In 1939 He purchased the New Joyce Hotel and hired his brother as manager. (The hotel no longer exists and his part of the Hilton parking lot now). In the mid 1950's he set his sites on Hawaii and invested in Honolulu Rapid Transit Company (HRT) better known to us as the Bus. In the 1960's he owned the controlling interest and was elected Chairman of the board, later he owned 95% of the stock. The press labeled him the moniker "Honolulu Harry". The HRT bus was later purchased by the City and County of Honolulu. He already owned much of the transport in New York City, as well as being a large real estate owner in Baltimore Maryland, Dallas Texas, Scranton Pennsylvania, Grand Rapids and a sprinkling of small holdings in several states. He steadily purchased stock in publicly traded stock, in these companies he was hoping to earn a seat on the respective boards and push business strategies to more profitable ventures. In the process he came to own massive amounts of real estate in Hawaii. He developed melanoma, requiring regular blood transfusions for the remainder of his life. In 1959, Harry and Jeanette set up a non-profit foundation, that would make grants to Jewish and non-Jewish charities in the US and Israel. The value was about $2 billion. Harry Weinberg died at age 82 in 1990, and he and his wife Jeannette are buried in Baltimore Maryland. Many people benefit from his fortune some in Israel and some in Hawaii.

Rudolf Bultmann (473)

Rudolf Karl Bultmann was born 20 August 1884 in Wiefelstede, German Empire, and son of a Lutheran minister. Following his father, he too became a Lutheran Theologian and Professor at the University of Marburg, He married Helene Feldmann on 6 August 1917; they had three daughters, and after 56 years of marriage Helene died in 1973. Following some brief lectureships at Breslau and Giessen, Bultmann returned to Marburg in 1921 as a full professor and stayed there until his retirement in 1951. His doctoral students included Hans Jonas, Ernst Kasemann, Gunter Bornkamm, Helmut Koester, and Ernst Fuchs. From 1933 until the end of the Second World War in 1945 he took into his family Uta Ranke-Heinemann, who had fled the bombs of Essen, and became friends with Martin Heidegger who taught at Marburg. Heidegger's views on existentialism had an influence on Bultmann's thinking. What arose from this friendship was a "sort of comradery" grounded on an active and open dialogue between Bultmann and Heidegger from 1923 to 1928; however, Bultmann himself stated that his views could not simply be reduced to Heideggerian categories in that "the New Testament is not a doctrine about our authentic existence as human beings, but a proclamation of this liberating act of God. He was critical of Nazism from the beginning and his career from 1933 to 1945 was marked by struggles with Nazis regarding their influence upon the universities and the Protestant Church. He taught that the Lutheran Church could not expect the Nazi State to be Christian, but he did not directly denounce its anti-Semitism. (In my personal opinion I believe theologians in Switzerland, the Netherlands, and some in Germany like Dietrich Bonhoeffer, did not bow to that evil philosophy, and the required Swastika was never displayed in many of these churches.) Although Bultmann strongly objected to the claim that Nazis had authority over all aspects of German life he rejected the Aryan paragraph that disenfranchised racially Jewish people including clergy with Jewish ancestry from civic organizations. He stated that this was incompatible with the essence of the Christian Church that makes no distinction between Jew and Gentile. He joined the confessing church, a movement that arose in opposition to the Pro Nazi Reich Church. Bultmann received honorary doctorates from many universities, for his outstanding teaching career. On 30 July 1976 he died at age 91in Marburg, he made a difference.

Karl Barth (474)

Karl Barth was born 10 May, 1886 in Basel Switzerland and burst on the scene with his commentary *The Epistle to the Romans* in the summer of 1916 while he was still a pastor in Stafenwil, immediately gaining him world wide attention; it was published in several languages, and got him invited to teach at the University of Gottingen. In the commentary he argues that the God who is revealed in the life, death, and resurrection of Jesus challenges and overthrows any attempt to ally God with human cultures, or human achievements. In 1934 the Protestant Church attempted to come to terms with the Third Reich, and Barth wrote *the Barmen Declaration* in which he rejected the influence of Nazism on German Christianity by arguing that the church's allegiance to the God of Jesus Christ, and must resist the influence of other lords, such as the *Fuhrer Adolph Hitler*. It was one of the founding documents of the Confessing Church and Barth was elected a member of its leadership council, *the Bruderrat*. He was forced to resign from his professorship at the University of Bonn in 1935 for refusing to swear an oath to Hitler. He then returned to his native Switzerland where he assumed a chair in systematic theology at the University of Basel. In the course of his appointment, he was required to answer a routine question if he supported the national defense. *Yes*, especially on the northern border. The newspaper *Neue Zurcher Zeitung* carried his criticism of the Nazis. He wrote a letter declaring that soldiers who fought against *the Third Reich* were serving a Christian cause. As a Swiss Calvinist theologian, he had significant influence on such people as Dietrich Bonhoeffer, Rudolf Bultmann, Thomas F. Torrance and others. His theology is most clear in his five-volume *magnum opus*, the Doctrine of the Word of God, widely regarded his most important theological work, *the Church Dogmatics*; it represents the pinnacle of his achievement as a theologian. It contains six million words, 9,000 pages in five volumes: the Doctrine of the Word of God, the Doctrine of God, the Doctrine of Creation, the Doctrine of Reconciliation, and the Doctrine of Redemption. In 1962, he visited the US and lectured at Princeton Theological Seminary, the University of Chicago, The Union Theological Seminary, and the San Francisco Theological Seminary. He was invited to be a guest at the Second Vatican Council, but his health did not permit him to attend, he did meet Pope Pius XII who said: Barth was the greatest theologian since Thomas Aquinas. Barth was featured on the cover of Time magazine April 20, 1962. One day before his death he wrote this for his followers: Don't be down hearted, things are not ruled from Moscow, or in Washington, or from Peking but things are ruled even here on earth entirely from heaven above. On December 10, 1968 he died at his home in Basel.

Gerrit Cornelis Berkouwer (475)

Gerrit Cornelis Berkouwer was born 8 June 1903 in Amsterdam, He was raised in Zaandam and in 1927 he and Catharina, Cornelia, Elisabeth Rippen was married in Den Haag. In 1932 he obtained his doctorate from the Free University in Amsterdam. His dissertation was entitled *Faith and Revelation in recent German theology*. In 1949 the first volume of his eighteen volume *Studies in Dogmatics* appeared in the Netherlands. In 1962 he was an observer at the second Vatican Council in Rome. His primary foreign influence has been in the Reformed Churches of North America where much of his writings are translated and published with a continues flow of seminary graduates to study under him for the degree of Doctor of Theology. Altogether Berkouwer mentored about 46 students who received the Th.D. degree; one of them was Rev. Deenik in New Zealand who was a very personal friend; he had come out of those war years in Europe and his church asked me to give him driving lessons. Here is how we did that. He was preaching and teaching in 3 or 4 cities in New Zealand in a range of several hundred miles. I had him drive under my supervision and if he was too tired, I would drive him to his destination. He learned driving techniques from me and I learned a lot of theology from him and in the process got to know much of Berkouwer's teachings, who got his seminary post at the Free University in Amsterdam during, and after, the Nazi occupation of World War II in which the Dutch National community suffered much from that occupation culminating in the Hunger Winter of 1944. Berkouwer's teachings came under serious criticism from professors like Klaas Schilder and a few others who organized themselves with a group of pastors of like-minded thoughts. These issues did not resolve, resulting in a split-off group who organized themselves as the "*Liberated Churches*". Later, Berkouwer indicated regret and thought the issue could have been handled differently and solutions keeping unity should have been found. In his writings he expressed an open mind that allowed developing friendship with Hendrikus Berkhof, the leading professor of systematics in the Nederland's Hervormde Kerk from which the Gereformeerde Kerken had split-off. Besides the studies in Dogmatics Berkouwer is known for his two books on Roman Catholicism *Conflict with Rome* (1948) and *Second Vatican Council and the New Catholicism*. Although he wrote more than 17 scholarly hard cover books, some written bilingual, one that stands out is his book written in the English language: "*Two hundred years of Theology, a report of a personal journey*. In 1953 he became a member of the Royal Netherlands Academy of Arts and Sciences. Professor Gerrit Berkouwer died at age 92 on 26 January 1996 in Voorhout, Netherlands.

Herman Boerhaave (476)

Herman Boerhaave was born 31 December 1668 in Voorhout, Holland. His father was a Protestant pastor. He was offered a scholarship at the University of Leiden. There he got a master's degree in philosophy, with a dissertation titled:" *The difference of the mind from the body*." In there he attacked the doctrines of Epicurus, (a respectable Greek Philosopher who lived 3 centuries BC), and others. He had no interest in many years of debates, changed direction and turned to study medicine, got his medical doctorate in 1693 In 1701 he was appointed lecturer on the institutes of medicine at Leiden, in his inaugural he recommended to his students Hippocrates as their model. In 1709 he became professor of botany and medicine and in that capacity, he did improvements to the botanic garden of Leiden authored numerous works descriptive of new species of plants. On 14 September, 1710 he married Maria Drolenvaux the daughter of a rich merchant. They had 4 children of only one daughter lived to adulthood. In 1714 he was appointed rector of the university and was chair of practical medicine, in this capacity he introduced the modern system of clinical instruction. Four years later he was appointed to the chair of chemistry as well. 1728 he was elected into the French Academy of Sciences and two years later in to the Royal Society of London. In 1729 declining health obliged him to resign the chairs of chemistry and botany. His reputation increased the fame of the University of Leiden, especially as a school of medicine that it became popular with visitors from every part of Europe. Most princes of Europe send pupils to him who found this skilful professor not only an indefatigable teacher, but also an affectionate guardian. Peter de Great (*credited for bringing Russia in to the modern age)*, took lessons from Boerhaave, Carl Linnaeus, and Voltaire traveled to visit him his reputation was not confined to Europe, a Chinese mandarin sent him a letter addressed to: "The illustrious Boerhaave, Physician of Europe." It still reached him. The operating theatre of the University of Leiden in which he once worked as an anatomist is now at the center of a museum named after him. From 1955 to 1961 his image was printed on Dutch 20-guilder banknotes. He was a devout Christian who often wrote about God in his work. He made many medical contributions in his lifetime devotion to finding cures for the human body. His insights aroused great interest among medical thinkers. As a professor at Leiden, he produced many textbooks and his lectures were circulated throughout the world. His chemistry textbook *Elementia Chemia* published in 1732 is world renown. On 23 September, 1738 at age 69 he died and is known as the Founder of clinical teaching. The Leiden University medical center organized training called: *Boerhaave Courses*.

Winsome Sears (477)

Winsome Earle Sears was born March 11 1964 in Kingston Jamaica; at her age six; the family immigrated to the US with their entire fortune of $1.75. Her father took whatever job he could find, and continued his education. They lived in the Bronx, N.Y. City. She served as an electrician in the United States Marines, and is married to a Marine Corps veteran with 2 daughters. She earned an A.A. from Tidewater Community College, a B.A. in English from Old Dominion University and an M.A. in organizational leadership from Regent University. Before she ran for public office, Sears ran a homeless shelter, and owns an appliance and plumbing repair store in Virginia. In November 2001, she upset 20-year Democratic incumbent Billy Robinson while running for the 90th district seat in Virginia's House of Delegates becoming the first Jamaican female Republican, first female veteran, and first naturalized citizen delegate to serve in that body. In 2004, Sears unsuccessfully challenged Democrat Bobby Scott for Virginia's 3rd congressional seat. She received 31% of the vote. She had high goals but was a lady of strong principles with clear priorities. In 2004 she took leave of politics to care for a daughter with bipolar disorder who died in a car crash along with Sears's two young granddaughters; she and her family live in Winchester Virginia. After a period of rest, she resumed her activities and became vice president of the Virginia Board of Education and received presidential appointments to the US Department of Veterans Affairs and the US Census Bureau. In September 2018, Sears entered the race for US Senate as a write-in candidate; she received 1% of the vote. This lady had amazing determination and never stopped trying. On May 11, 2021 Sears won the Republican nomination for Lieutenant Governor of Virginia on the 5th ballot. On November 2, 2021 she won the race on a ticket with gubernatorial candidate Glenn Youngkin, becoming the first black woman elected to a statewide office in Virginia. In her victory speech she made this profound statement and said: "When I joined the Marine Corps, I was still a Jamaican; but this country has done so much for me, I was willing to die for this country." She is expected to be inaugurated as the 42nd lieutenant governor of Virginia on January 25, 2022. On a November 21, 2021 on CNN's "State of the Union" Sears refused to acknowledge whether she'd received the Covid-19 vaccine, citing healthcare privacy and personal information. She called for government officials to allow individuals to decide for themselves what precautionary measures to take to protect against the COVID-19 virus and said she would never force anyone to get such a vaccine. If she was not foreign born, (which makes her constitutionally ineligible), but with her leadership qualities and political aspirations she belongs in the White House.

Frank E. Midkiff (478)

Frank Elbert Midkiff was born 15 November 1887 in Anna Illinois; his parents were Reverend James and Bertha Wilson Midkiff. He was the fourth of nine children. At his young age of twelve his mother died. For any child it is difficult to lose a mom just as you enter the teenage years. He went to Stonington High School, Shutleff Academy and College in Upper Alton Illinois. There he worked for a short time as foreman at Kimberly Gold Mine in Jardine Montana, but did not stay there long. Between his junior and senior year at Colgate College, he worked as a coach at Lewistown High School, to earn money for his college tuition from 1908 to 1910; he taught chemistry, biology, and Roberts Rules of Order, (parliamentary procedures). From 1911 to 1912 he got a Phi Beta Kappa A. B. in Geology. In Highstown New Jersey he was an English teacher and coach of baseball, football, and athletic director for boys. Then he moved to Hawaii where he worked as a teacher at Oahu College, (in 1934 the school's name was changed to Punahou School). In 1917 he married Ruth Richard who was the daughter of the principal of Kamehameha Schools, and they had three children: Mary, Robert and Frances. Midkiff served in the United States Army during World War I. When the war ended, he received an honorable discharge and joined the firm Lewers and Cooke Ltd. In 1923 he was appointed to the board of trustees of Kamehameha Schools was elected their president serving in that capacity to 1934. He earned his Ph. D in Education from Yale University in 1935. Living in Hawaii he served as acting president of the Honolulu Chamber of Commerce, and President Dwight Eisenhower appointed him High Commissioner of the Trust Territory of the Pacific Islands. Frank was a member of the Pacific War Memorial and served as president from 1918 to 1928. He was elected chairman of Bishop Memorial Church at Kamehameha schools, and was a life member of the Bernice Pauahi Bishop Museum, which was founded by Mr. Bishop in honor of his wife Bernice Pauahi. The Frank E Midkiff learning center was founded in *his* honor in January 1977. He was an Eagle Scout and sponsor of the Aloha council of Boy Scouts of America, charter member of the Honolulu YMCA, and Midkiff held memberships in the Honolulu Academy of Arts, The Outdoor Circle, Armed Services YMCA, Outrigger Canoe club, the Waialae Country Club, and the Pacific Club. He is the author of *Survey of Education in American Samoa*, in addition to *that* he authored several pamphlets and numerous articles in professional trade journals; and was a member of The Red Cross, and Central Union Church. Frank E. Midkiff died in Honolulu on August 7, 1983. The learning center at the Kamehameha School is his legacy; he was an American educator and a civic leader.

Ruddy F. Tongg (479)

Ruddy Tongg was born in 1905, graduated from the University of Hawaii and after college in 1925 became a Successful Chinese American businessman. He started a bi-lingual Chinese weekly that eventually grew into *Tongg Publishing Company*, the company did well, but Ruddy had a dream to start an airline company in Hawaii; with waves of returning GI's, the war had ended in 1945, the world changed and Hawaii was changing rapidly. It is an Island state, the only connection between Islands was by water transport, or by Hawaiian Airline who had begun in 1929 and had no competitor. Tongg had been re-buffed a few times when he was trying to fly to another Island, which made him more determined to fill the need for a *people's airline*. Tongg felt the void of a healthy competitor was a great risk for future inter island travel; after all, the Hawaii business climate was already dominated by the big five Oligopoly. With a local HUI of like-minded investors, they purchased a few DC-10 surplus aircraft and founded Trans Pacific Air in 1946 just one year after World War II had ended. The company was not certified for regular scheduled flights; therefore, Trans Pac Air could only operate charter flights. Their application for such certification was fiercely opposed by Hawaiian airline, but Tongg's entrepreneurial spirit overcame all odds and in 1949 TPA was certified. He assembled a management team that built a struggling airline company in to a successful enterprise. When initially lack of financial resources threatened the survival of this young company, Tongg turned to his Chinese friend Dr Hung Wo Ching who got the required capital, and became president of the company. With the infusion of cash and support of Hawaii's tourist-economy, the airline literally took off and changed its name to *Aloha Airline*. But then in the mid 1980 a newcomer arrived "*Mid Pacific Air*" who began inter island travel, operating low-cost air service between the islands. At that time, I was active in the business community in Hawaii and *word down the grapevine* was that the company is not here to serve the local community but will only last till one of the three airlines is driven out by economic necessity. And *Mid Pacific Air* seemed to have the required capital to stay in the air. Out of sheer principle I refused to use that company and felt Aloha had hired primarily local people and many of my friends worked for Aloha Air, and as a regular outer Island traveler I did not fly on *Mid Pacific Air*. That airline ended its service in Hawaii closing its operation on January 19. 1998 and *Aloha Air* did not survive and suspended its operation on March 30, 2008. Ruddy Tongg was a polo player with his pony "*Lovely Sage*". Ruddy Tongg did not have to witness the demise of his dream airline. He lived to age 83 and died in 1988, twenty years before his dream airline went bankrupt.

Stanley Kennedy (480)

Stanley Carmichael Kennedy was born July 7, 1890 in Honolulu in the Kingdom of Hawaii. King Kalakaua had died and Queen Lili'uokalani came to the throne when Stanley was one year old. He attended Punahou School, graduating in 1908, then went to Stanford University and graduated in 1912. In 1914 Kennedy joined the navy when the US entered the war. He was sent to the Massachusetts institute of technology for naval officers training then to Naval Air station in Pensacola. There he earned his wings, and was sent to England flying the Curtiss-H16 Seaplanes patrolling the North Sea to spot German submarines. On one mission, Kennedy and his crew went on patrol 7 hours and 59 minutes setting a world record for sustained flight earning him the Navy's citation Star/Silver Star. After World War I he returned to his career at the Inter-Island Steam Navigation Company. His experience flying sea-planes led him to the possibility of using seaplanes to connect the people of Hawaii. He approached his father about that, but he saw airplanes as flying toys, only useful in good weather. Kennedy became president of Inter-Island of Steam Navigation Company from 1933 until it ceased operation in 1947. After he had returned from Stanford, he met Martha Davenport on an Inter-Island steamer while she was vacationing in Hawaii from her home in Chattanooga Tennessee. They wrote letters to each other and kept in contact. After the war Stanley stopped in Tennessee and the meeting of Martha was a blessing and the two seemed to be made for each other, got married and lived in Hawaii in a beachfront home just East of Honolulu, near Aina Haina, and had a weekend home in Kahuku on the North Shore of Oahu. He was president of Coca-Cola Bottling Company of Hawaii as well as the Honolulu Chamber of Commerce. However, he had a dream that had not come to fruition and would not rest until there was air connection between the Islands in his home State. In 1929 he began a subsidiary of Inter Island Steam Navigation Company which became the forerunner of Inter Island Airways and in 1941 Hawaiian Airlines. The company began on October 6, 1929 providing sightseeing flights over Oahu. Scheduled service began a month later to Hilo with stops on Molokai and Maui; they phased out the older flying boats. Modern pressurized equipment was introduced in 1952. Stanley Kennedy was able to see his dream come true as Hawaiian Airlines became a major competitor on the world market with destinations in all the Hawaiian Islands as well as several Asia-Pacific countries and territories operating a fleet of 61 aircraft flying to 32 foreign destinations such as South Korea, Tahiti, New Zealand Australia, Japan and others. Kennedy lived to age 77 and died on April 19, 1968 and was buried in Oahu cemetery.

Miranda Devine (481)

Miranda Divine was born July 1, 1961 in New York City, and is the eldest daughter of Frank Devine, a New Zealand-born Australian Newspaper editor and journalist. Miranda attended school at Loreto Kirribilli in Sydney and the International School of the Sacred Heart Tokyo. She has a Master in Science in Journalism from Northwestern University (USA) and a Bachelor of Science in Mathematics from Macquarie University in Australia which is considered in the top 2% of universities around the world. Devine studied first-year architecture at Sydney University, but did not pursue that as a career; She joined the Boston Herald as a reporter and feature writer, and in 1989 as she joined the Daily Telegraph (a National British daily) as assistant editor, police reporter and columnist after returning to Australia; she had previously worked at the British tabloid _The Sun_ and the British newspaper _Sunday times_ in London. More recently she has focused on American politics; she published her columns in _the New York Post_ and makes appearances on local media promoting her material. She is very different from many major opinion columnists; Devine is more conservative and seems to be rather independent in expressing her opinions, very different from a large number of columnists, who in my judgment often echo each others liberal bias. Devine comes across to me as an original thinker, whether right or wrong she puts it out there, and her logic is mostly conservative. She opined in the Sydney morning Herald that the racial element of the Sydney gang rapes had been airbrushed out of media coverage and stated that the victims alleged that prosecutors had intentionally censored their official statements to remove mention of racially sensitive material. The Guardian and the Sidney Morning Herald have accused her of promoting the white genocide conspiracy theory described as pivotal in popularizing the concept within Australian politics. She has repeatedly claimed that climate change or Global warming is a political conspiracy. In another issue she has not been afraid to tackle the issue of Same Sex Marriage and argued that the 2011 riots in England were the result of a fatherless society. In October 2020, The Guardian described her as one of Trump's favorite writers, she is mine too; in 2015 she claimed that women abusing welfare were the main cause of domestic violence contending there is a welfare incentive for unsuitable women having children to a string of freckless men. I think we should import Miranda Devine to Honolulu she would be a healthy balance to our toxic un-opposed single-party political climate in Hawaii.

Noah Webster (482)

Noah Webster was born October 16, 1758, at West Hartford, Connecticut US. He was known for his extensive work as an American lexicographer, American Spelling Book, and his American dictionary of the English language, and was instrumental in giving American English a dignity and vitality of its own. He entered Yale in 1774, interrupted his studies to serve briefly in the American Revolution, and was graduated in 1778. For someone like me who came from a different language, his books were a necessity to have for survival in business here. Both his speller and dictionary reflected the principle that spelling, grammar, and usage should be based upon the living spoken language rather than on artificial roles. He made useful contributions as a teacher, grammarian, journalist, essayist, lecturer, and lobbyist. The absence of a federal copyright law until 1790 and discrepancies among the state laws left the author of a popular book open to piracy unless you exerted strenuous efforts. Webster's letters written to various legislatures reflect his activity on his own behalf; he traveled widely lobbying for uniform copyright laws lecturing, teaching, and giving singing lessons to help support himself. In 1787 he founded the short-lived _American Magazine_ in New York City; this publication combined criticism with essays on education, government, agriculture and a variety of other subjects. After his marriage in 1789, Webster practiced law in Hartford until 1703, when he founded in New York a pro-Federalist daily newspaper _the American Minerva_, and a semi-weekly paper, _The Herald_, which was made up of reprinted selections from the daily; he sold both papers in 1803. Webster wrote on many subjects: Politics (Sketches on American Policy 1785, sometimes called the first statement of the US Constitution), economics, medicine, physical science, and language. He noted the living language as he traveled but with varying degrees of approbation. According to the degree of correspondence between what he heard and what he himself used. He began his lifelong efforts to promote a distinctively American education. His first step in this direction was preparation of A Grammatical Institute of the English Language, the first part being _the American Spelling Book_ (1783), the famed "**_Blue Backed Speller,_**" which has never been out of print; it provided much of Webster's income for the rest of his life, its total sales have been estimated at 100 million copies or more. Webster spoke of American English as "Federal English" always contrasting the superior usage of the yeoman of America with the alleged affectations of London. Noah Webster died at age 84 on May 28 1843, in New Haven, Conn.

Theo H. Davies (483)

Theophilus Harris Davies was born 4 January, 1834 in Stourbridge Worcestershire England, son of a Welsh minister and his English wife. He was recruited in England to join the firm of Janion, Green and Co. in Hawaii, a successor to Starkey Janion and Co in 1845. Davies was an English businessman who had raised his capital mostly in England; he became the founder of Theo H. Davies and Co, one of Hawaii's big five sugar companies. Davies arrived in Hawaii in 1857 but stayed only till 1862 and returned to England. In 1867 Janion and Green were in financial trouble and Davies was brought back to Hawaii to reorganize the company and bail out Janion; he did so and by January 1868, Davies controlled the business and it was being operated as Theo H. Davies and Company. Under the laws of the Provisional Government it became Theo H. Davies and Company Limited in January 1894, and grew to one of Hawaii's "Big Five" sugar firms. In 1875 he refinanced the Honolulu Iron Works and hired Alexander Young, and partnered with Young in many future businesses; Janion had left the company he died in 1881.The business expended to add departments for steamship agents, grocery stores, dry goods, and hardware and later even car dealerships. Davies died in 1898 and Francis Mills Swanzy became managing director and T. Clive Davies (son of Theo) was a board member, and kept the family connection to the company. In 1917 T. Clive Davies and Ernest Hay Wodehouse were named co-managing directors but Davies died that same day. A new headquarters building, built in 1921 served through the 1960's; then a 32-story Davies Pacific Center was built at 841 Bishop Street. In 1928 the company opened a Manila branch and expanded with sugarcane plantations in the Philippines. John E Russell led the company until the 1950's. Geoffrey C. Davies (T. Clive's son) became chairman, followed by Gerald M. Wilkinson, James H. Tabor and others who served as presidents. Dillingham Corporation made a failed takeover attempt. Theo H. Davies and Co remained in family hands until 1973, when the family sold the company to Jardine, a Hong Kong based conglomerate. Davies became the first big five to get out of sugar. Jardine (the Hong Kong based company), later diversified its holdings, buying the franchises in Hawaii for restaurants as Pizza Hut, Taco Bell as well as auto dealerships; such as Mercedes-Benz and Jaguar. Starting 2003 Jardine gradually sold it various holdings in Hawaii. Theo H. Davies (manila) founded in 1928 currently exists as a separate holding company in Manila under a different name and is involved in education, insurance, shipping and overseas job placement businesses in Manila and other places in the Philippines.

Francis Mills Swanzy (484)

Francis Mills Swanzy was born 4 February 1850 in Dublin, Ireland, the son of John Swanzy and Margaret Francis Mills Swanzy. He was educated at Portora School in Enniskillen and at Science College in Dublin Ireland. When he finished school, he did what many other Europeans did and that was seek a better future and search FOR SOMETHING that might interest him; and booked passage on a ship for the long journey round the bottom of South America, and 6 weeks later disembarked in the Islands of Hawaii. He arrived in 1880 at age 30 full of youthful enthusiasm for the work to be accomplished in his new adopted home; he was well trained in business through his previous connection with several of the leading firms of Manchester and Liverpool in England. Immediately upon arrival he entered employment at Theo H. Davies and Co and very early in his career was interested in the Honolulu Iron Works which was owned by the company; he rose rapidly to a high position in both companies. Mr. Swanzy was known for his executive ability and from his early arrival his zeal and efficiency was evident the moment he took on a project, His keen business judgment and foresight made him an immediate success in whatever undertaking he was engaged in. Tireless in professional zeal he was always ready to take on additional business and carry them to success, and only ten years after he arrived in Hawaii, he became a partner in Theo H. Davies and Co, and when the firm was incorporated in 1894, he was named a director Mr. Davies had died earlier. In 1887 he married Miss Julie Judd, former chamberlain to King Kalakaua. He was elected president of the Honolulu Iron Works Company in 1904 and in the next 12 years assumed the presidency of the Waiakea Mill Company, Sugar Factors company, Lapahoehoe sugar Co, Kaiwiki Sugar Company Ltd, Kukaiau Planation Co. Ltd, Hamakua Mill Company, Kaeleku Sugar Co Ltd, Papaloa Agricultural Co Ltd, Paauilo Agricultural Company Ltd, Pearl City Fruit Co Ltd, and Waianae Lime Co. Francis mills Swanzy was an industrial builder, a leader in the great sugar industry of Hawaii and one of the outstanding men in the development of various mercantile industries. In all the years Francis Mills Swanzy was here he emerged as one of the greatest business leaders and led Theo H. Davies to the position of being one of the largest companies in Hawaii. He was an executive that knew how to manage and make vital decisions, it is a trait that few people have. He died in Honolulu at age 67 on February 26, 1917, his story was published by the Honolulu Star Bulletin in 1925.

Alexander Young (485)

Alexander Young was born December 14, 1833 in Blackburn Scotland, son of Robert and Agnes; Alexander apprenticed as a mechanical engineer at Alexander Chaplin and Co in Glasgow and later at Anderson and Company in London. He married Ruth Pearce in early 1860. One of his first jobs was sailing around the Horn in 1860 to Vancouver Island with a shipload of machinery to built and operate a large sawmill in Alberni. He and his wife and one child left there and set sail for the Sandwich Islands on Feb. 5, 1865, they later had nine surviving children. In the Sandwich Islands, he formed a partnership with William Lidgate to operate a foundry at Hilo Hawaii, and during that time the sugar business expanded substantially in the Islands. Moving to Honolulu he bought the interest of Thomas Hughes in Honolulu Iron Works. Theo H. Davies had invested money in the company and asked Young to manage it, especially after a devastating fire in 1860. Young accepted its management and stayed there for the next 32 years as well as invested in Sugar Plantation Enterprises, and in that endeavor became president of the Waikea Mill Company. In 1887 he became a citizen of Hawaii and during the Monarchy he served in the House of Nobles In 1839. He had been a member of the advisory council under the provincial government and was a minister of Interior in President Dole's Cabinet. In 1900, he formed the Von Hamm Young Company; principals were Young's son Archibald Alfred and son in law Conrad Carl Von Hamm. One of their early projects was constructing a 192 Room Hotel Building on the corner of King and Bishop Street, naming it the *Alexander Young Hotel*; the location was near perfect right in downtown Honolulu completed in 1903. In 1905 Young acquired the Ala Moana Hotel and later the in *Honolulu Royal Hawaiian Hotel*, which became the Army and Navy YMCA. At the time of construction, the Alexander Young Hotel was *the hotel* in the entire Pacific, there was nothing that compared. It was a visitor's stop for 400,000 tourists and the Alexander Young is where everyone wanted to be. The 2nd floor of the 4-story building was dominated by military occupancy. He had on the 5th floor a well manicured roof garden. Later the sons took over the business; he had done his best to accommodate the visitor industry, but the downtown hotel building did not offer the natural beauty of Hawaii beaches as Waikiki did. The Company expanded to include automobile dealerships in the 1920's. After Von Ham's death in 1965 the company eventually liquidated in one of Hawaii's first bankruptcy cases. The hotel building was purchased by the army in 1917, and in 1981 it was demolished, and later replaced by the Pacific Trade Center Building on Bishop Square. Alexander Young died July 2, 1910, and is recognized as the father of the hotel business in Hawaii.

William Wrigley Jr. (486)

William Wrigley Jr. was born on September 30, 1861 in Philadelphia, Pennsylvania, the son of Mary Ann Ladley and William Mills Wrigley Sr. He moved from Philadelphia to Chicago, and started a business there. All he had was $32 to his name (In 2021 money $931), and started Wrigley's Scouring Soap. He offered customers small premiums, some baking powder as an incentive to buy his soap. Finding the baking powder was more popular than his soap, he learned fast, and switched to selling baking powder and giving his customers two packages of chewing gum for each can of baking powder they purchased. He learned a new lesson again and found that the premium he offered was more popular than the base product, and his company began to concentrate on the manufacture and the sale of chewing gum, and it was in *that* business Wrigley made his name and fortune. He was instrumental in the development of the island of Catalina 24 mile of the coast of Long Beach California. (In 1962 we made a visit there going over by sea-plane flying out of Long Beach Airport by the Catalina Flying boat, landing in the ocean near the Avalon Casino, and returning by Ferry to San Pedro). Wrigley had bought a controlling interest in the Island in 1919. He improved the Island with public utilities, new steamships, a hotel, the Casino building, 26 miles of road with the intent of making a movie in 1924, a few Bisons were brought in, these have since multiplied and are 100 to 150 buffalos are now roaming wild. He did extensive plantings of trees, shrubs and flowers, and sought to create an enterprise that would employ the local residents by the use of minerals that were found on the beach near Avalon casino, and create an industry with the craft and sale of pottery in order for the local people to create an industry that would support them. In 1927 he created the Pebbly Beach quarry and tile plant, after building the Avalon Casino in 1929, the Catalina clay products began producing pottery, clay products, glazed tiles, dinnerware and other household items and souvenirs such as bookends. In 1972, his son Philip established a plan for the future of Catalina Island and opened the Wrigley Botanical gardens on the island. The Wrigley district in Long Beach California also bears his name. In 1916 he bought a minority stake in the Chicago Cubs baseball team. In 1930, Wrigley gave the Salvation Army use of his six-story factory building he owned in Chicago. It could be used as a lodging house for the unemployed. He converted the Arizona Biltmore Hotel into a winter cottage in 1931; at 16,000 square feet it was the smallest of his five residences. He died at age 70 in Arizona on January 26, 1932 and left his fortune to his daughter Dorothy and his son Philip. One of his mansions in Pasadena California is now the headquarters of the tournament of Roses Parade.

Chris Gardner (487)

Christopher Paul Gardner was born Feb. 9, 1954 in Milwaukee Wisconsin to Thomas and Bettye Jean Gardner. He was a second child and the only boy born to Bettye Jean. His older half-sister Ophelia is from a previous union to Freddie. Chris did not have many positive role models as a child. His father was living in another state, and his other sisters are from his mother's previous marriage. His stepfather was physically abusive to his birth mother and to his sisters. In one instance his mother was put in prison when Freddie falsely accused her of welfare fraud she was cleared when it was proven that the charge was made up. During her prison time the children lived in foster care, and again a little later when their mother was accused of trying to kill Freddie. In Foster care he discovered he three maternal uncles, Archibald, Willie, and Henry. Of the three, Henry had the most profound influence on his life, he entered his life at age 8 when he most needed a father figure; but Henry drowned in the Mississippi river when Chris was 9 years old; at the funeral he learned that mom was again in prison when she came escorted by a prison guard. She was a positive source in his life and encouraged him saying: "*Chris, believe in you-self and be self-reliant.*" He took that to heart, and was determined to avoid: Illiteracy, Alcoholism, and Domestic abuse. He did well as a medical salesman, and tracked down his father, and bought the Red Ferrari of Michael Jordan, only changed the number plate to "Not MJ" He embarked on a medical career, but abandoned that after he saw a well-dressed man, who was a stockbroker, and applied with Merryll Lynch, Payne Webber, Dean Witter, Smith Barney and others. He trained with E.F. Hutton, upon completion he came to work on the first day to discover that his manager had been fired, and his relationship with Jackie was deteriorating they had a child, when he tried to get his child from Jackie, she fell in to the bushes got scratched, and Chris was detained. A policeman saw it and the judge ordered him to be confined 10 days. His car accumulated $1,200 in parking fees upon release he found his apartment empty, and Jackie was gone. He dedicated himself to his children and was the speaker at his daughter's graduation. He wrote his life story in an autobiography, offered it to Hollywood, they liked it, and made a motion picture of his life titled; *the pursuit of happiness*, which grossed $163 million domestically and $300 million worldwide. He received the Father of the Year award from NFI as well as other awards. His story gave me a new awareness of the foster boys that grew up in our home, realizing anew the importance of a stable intact family. Chris, as a black man, with all odds against him, succeeded and if he could, then anyone can.

Bruce Olson (488)

Bruce was born on November 10, 1941 and raised in a Lutheran Scandinavian environment in Minnesota, at age 19 he felt God's call to minister; he had been touched by missionaries who reported on their ministry to the Indians in the jungles of South America. He got educated, prepared, and studied Hebrew and Greek, was driven to his knees seeking direction. He did not get support from his denomination but was convinced this was the call of God. He began to attend an interdenominational church and followed his heart; I read his book *Bruchko* at least 25 years ago, and it is still one of the better and most riveting books I have read. I used to travel and often flew these long-distance flights, like 14 hours in the air, even as a slow reader, I could read an entire book in one flight, his book is one of those you can not put it down. He did become a missionary quite different from those who have stopped for R & R at our home during the 60 years we have lived in Honolulu. He traveled to South America, at first was a little disappointed with the cool reception of other missionaries, but eventually set out for the jungle and found the Yuka Indians, spent many months with them, then went in search of the Motilone tribes; when he found them at first, they almost killed him. He endured surviving all the parasites of jungle life. Instead of turning back, such trials emboldened him to stay. He had learned that the Bible teaches we should take joy in the Lords work even during suffering. He went fishing with the men and eventually his body adjusted to living in the jungle. He befriended Bobby, a young warrior and one of the leaders. He learned their customs, diet, culture, and language till he was one of them. But never lost his purpose, that was to bring the gospel to the tribe, he let the witch doctor treat him and converted him to more Western medicine. It was Bobby (a name Bruce gave him) who was one of his first converts. Bobby could sing and chant, and was a family man with a wife and children, but sadly he was killed by his own people. God blest the efforts of Bruce, the entire tribe was converted to Christianity and Bruce was able to translate much of the Bible in their local language. His mission trip turned into a 30-year endeavor that never ended. The Motilone tribe lives on the borders of Venezuela and Colombia. There have been violent clashes with oil company employees seeking to drill on their land. Olson received international attention when he was kidnapped by the National Liberation Army of Colombia on 24 October 1988. The ELN judged him in the revolutionary system and found him guilty of exploiting the Motilone Indians. He was condemned to die, and his execution was planned to be carried out on July 6, 1989. Bruchko sold more than 300,000 copies and Olson is alive and lives on the Colombia/Venezuela border where he wants to be.

D. Howard Hitchcock (489)

David Howard Hitchcock was born May 15, 1861 in Hilo Hawaii. His father served in the legislature of the Hawaiian Kingdom and his sister Almeda was the first <u>woman lawye</u>r in Hawaii. After graduating from Punahou and Oberlin College in Ohio, he saw his first art exhibition. Back in Hawaii he wondered the Volcano wilderness with a sketch pad making scenic oils and watercolors. French artist Jules Tavernier, saw his sketches, and convinced him to study art seriously. He took that advice, and studied at the National Academy of Design in New York City from 1891 to 1893, then returned to Hawaii. In 1894 he became one of the founders of the Kilohana Art League, (an active art program in Honolulu at the turn of the century exhibiting at least twice a year.) He married Hester Judd Dickson on June 16, 1898 at the Cathedral Church of St Andrew, in Honolulu. Her maternal grandfather was Gerrit Parmele Judd, an early missionary-physician to Hawaii. During extensive travels in the 1900s, Hitchcock explored the volcanic regions in the island of Hawaii, and in July 1907 he made his first visit to the island of Kauai where he painted Waimea Canyon. In 1915 he toured the island of Maui. He was a leading member of <u>Hawaii's Volcano School</u> and his most important painting dates were from 1905 to 1930. In 1909 his paintings were exhibited in the Alaska-Yukon-Pacific Exposition in Seattle, where he was awarded a prize. In June 1910 he sailed for California and painted for several weeks around Mill Valley in Marin County. In July he held a one-man exhibition at Schussler Brothers Gallery in San Francisco and received positive reviews in the *San Francisco Call*. He spent the remainder of July and August in Carmel-by-the-Sea, in California where he painted and exhibited his oils and watercolors at the Fourth Annual of the Carmel Arts and Crafts Club. Thereafter he traveled to Los Angeles and the East Coast to display his paintings. From 1912 to 1924 he had several displays there, and then returned to San Francisco in 1924 to exhibit at several commercial Galleries, including Vickery, Atkins and Torrey, the St Francis Hotel, and Rabjon and Morcom. His was also included in the art galleries at San Francisco's Panama- Pacific International Exposition of 1915. In 1919 he painted two murals for the Pan-Pacific Union in Honolulu. In 1924 his canvases were displayed in the First Hawaiian and South Seas Exhibition in the Los Angeles as well as in the Golden Gate International Exposition in San Francisco and at the 1939 New York World Fair. He witnessed the attack on Pearl Harbor in 1941. He had 3 children, is credited with bringing Boy Scouting to Hawaii and became the first scoutmaster in Honolulu. His reflective painting impressions of the Hawaii Volcanoes in Oil and Watercolor are profound. He died at age 81 on January 1 1943 in Honolulu.

Bob Dole (490)

Robert Joseph Dole was born July 22, 1923 in Russell Kansas US. Bob graduated from Russell High School in 1941 and went to the University of Kansas; he had been a star high school athlete, in college he joined the Kappa Sigma fraternity and served on the basket ball and football team. In 1942 he saw the NAZI aggression in Europe as well that of Japan in the Pacific; when Bob understood the need for American military intervention on two fronts, he enlisted and offered his service in defense of the fatherland; Bob was committed to do what he could. He became a Lieutenant and his unit was sent to Italy where he fought Nazi aggression in Alpine Balogna in Italy, there he was hit by a German shell wounding his upper back and right arm shattering his collar bone and part of his spine, he said he lay face down in the dirt and could see nothing. When his fellow soldiers saw him, they gave him the largest dose of morphine they dared to do. He was transported in paralyzed condition to Kansas where he was expected to die. He survived, but was never totally normal again, and went back to what he loved to do which was being an American politician and attorney who represented Kansas in the United States Senate, prior to that he served four terms in the US House of Representatives having won his first election in 1960; in 1968 he was elected to the senate where he served as chairman of the Republican National Committee from 1971 to 1973 and chairman of the Senate Finance Committee from 1981 to 1985. He led the Senate Republicans from 1985 to his resignation in 1996. He was Senate majority leader from 1985 to 1987 and again from 1995 to 1996. In that role he helped defeat Democratic President Bill Clinton's Health Care Plan. President Gerald Ford chose Dole as his running mate in the 1976 election, after Vice President Nelson Rockefeller withdrew from completing his term. In 1996 Dole won the Republican nomination and selected Jack Kemp as his running mate; The Republican ticket lost the General Election to Bill Clinton, making Dole the first unsuccessful major party nominee for both president and vice president. He resigned from the US Senate during the 1996 campaign and did not seek public office again after that election. He married Phyllis Holden in 1948 and divorced in 1972. He met Elizabeth in 1972 and they were married in December 1975. In 2001 at age 77 he had a successful procedure after an abdominal aneurysm. He always remained good natured about his heath. After a distinguished legislative career Bob Dole at age 98 died on Sunday December 05, 2021. He was a towering leader who lived a life that speaks of character, patriotism, and lifetime commitment to Veterans, he never forgot his fellow soldiers, civilian or military; Bob Dole was an American Hero in more ways than one.

Hans Wilsdorf (491)

Hans Wilsdorf was born 22 March 1881 in Kulmbach, German Empire, to Anna and Johan Daniel Ferdinand Wilsdorf and was the second son of a family of 3 children. His mother died when he was very young, and his father died soon after, making Hans an orphan at age 12. His fate was in the hands of his uncles who sold the family business which had belonged to his grandfather and later to his father. Hans and his brother and sister were sent to excellent boarding schools where they received superb educations. Wilsdorf published his autobiography in 1946 in a 4-volume set, in there he stated: "Our uncles were not indifferent to our fate, but made us become self-reliant very early in life, I believe that much of my success is due to those years." Hans excelled in mathematics and languages, and in 1900 began his career in Swiss watch making, (although he had moved to La Chaux-de-Fonds to work as an English Correspondent and be a part time clerk with the watch firm of Messrs. Cuno Korten, and Leoppold Robert, where he was paid a salary of 80 Swiss Francs.) The company exported around one million Francs worth of pocket watches annually. Cuno Korten worked with all grades of watches, as well as manufactured a few from the ground up. His responsibility was winding hundreds of pocket watches as well as verifying that all watches were accurate. Wilsdorf gained tremendous insight into watch-making as well as acquired valuable knowledge about how all types of watches were produced. In 1903, he moved to London England where he worked for a superior watch making company, and in 1905, he set up a business with Alfred Davis, with its goal to produce high quality timepieces at affordable prices. In 1958 Wilsdorf shares this story from his past: "In 1905 I was sitting on the upper level of a double-decker powered by horses in London and a good genie whispered in my ear the name "_Rolex_"; a few days later the Rolex brand was filed and officially registered in Switzerland by Wilsdorf and Davis. In 1914, (only a decade after Wilsdorf had moved to London), just before the assassination of Archduke Ferdinand in Sarajevo which triggered the beginning of World War I, Rolex was the first wristwatch in history to be awarded a Class A certificate from the Kew Observatory. The company grew quickly and in no time, Rolex had 40 employees. That year Wilsdorf wrote: "My personal opinion is that pocket watches will soon disappear and be replaced by wrist watches." By 1915 the British government hit Rolex with 33% duty, prompting Rolex in 1919 to move its headquarters to Geneva Switzerland, where it remains to this day. Hans Wilsdorf legacy and contribution in horology is unparalleled. He died at age 79 on 6 July 1960 and was buried in Kings Cemetery in Geneva Switzerland.

Leo Terrell (492)

Leo Terrell was born February 1, 1955 in southern California, and was educated at Gardena High School of Harbor Gateway Los Angeles graduating in 1972, and California State University graduating in 1977 with a BA. He taught high School history, geography and economics at Gage Middle School in Huntington Park, California. He holds a masters degree in education from Pepperdine University as well as a J. D. degree from the UCLA School of Law. On December 4, 1990 Leo Terrell became a member of the California Bar. He was Chairman of the Black-Korean Alliance, an advisory Board Member for the U. S. Equal Employment Opportunity Commission (EEOC), especially in their work Against Hate Crimes. He wrote the book "*You're Rights at the workplace*" and "*the things your boss won't tell you in 1998.*" With former Los Angeles Superior Court Judge Burton Katz, Terrell co-hosted a weekday talk show: *Terrell and Katz;* it debuted on June 3, 1996 on KMPC Radio in Los Angeles. It was a point-counterpoint program with Terrell as the liberal voice and Katz the conservative. Starting October 5, 1996, the show moved to weekends. Terrell continued to host a weekend legal show on KABC until August 15, 2010 and remained a recurring guest host for KABC's *The Peter Tilden Show*. As of July 2021, Leo has returned to KABC with a new afternoon drive show called *Leo 2.0 Life @ 5*. Terrell has frequently appeared on Fox News programs such as The O'Reilly Factor and Hannity. In the earlier days Leo was a Liberal Democrat but in a July 2020 interview, he declared his support for President Donald Trump and for the first time declared his support for the Republican Party. Leo was a completely different man, and as viewers we needed to do a second take it was obvious something had happened to Leo. Terrell became a member of the NAACP in 1990 and did pro bono legal work for the organization. After he expressed support for Carolyn Kuhl a Los Angeles County judge nominated by George W. Bush to the United States Court of Appeals for the Ninth Circuit, whose nomination was filibustered in the US Senate, he left the NAACP and accused the organization of bullying him out. Office director Hillary O. Shelton responded: He's not an NAACP lawyer; he's done volunteer work for us,
We appreciate that, but when he takes a position that is diametrically opposed to ours, he's not speaking for us. Leo has appeared on Larry King live, ran for the seat of District 10 on the Los Angeles City Council but lost. Leo Terrell was a declared Democrat 1996-1920 and is a declared Republican 2020 to present.

Carlos Ott (493)

Carlos Ott was born October 16, 1946 in Montevideo in Uruguay and became a Uruguayan architect based in Canada. He graduated from the school of architecture at the University of the Republic Uruguay at the age of 23 in 1971, then he received a Fulbright Scholarship, with that he studied at the University of Hawaii, and Washington University graduating with a Masters in Urban design and Architecture in 1972. Then a miraculous event happened giving him world fame. A group of people in Paris had been discussing the idea of a new opera house that would be so unique it was to be unparalleled anywhere in the world; after all, Paris was a very special city, referred to as the city of love, the city of classical music, the city of Notre Dame Basilica, and the home of the Eiffel Tower. The location chosen was the old Bastille train station which had been slated for demolition anyway. With that distinction the group decided to ask 700 architects around the world for proposals; 744 responded; and to avoid the temptation of looking mostly at "*big name*" architects, all submitted entries were reviewed anonymously. The winner was a relatively unknown architect Carlos Ott from Uruguay which in 1983 made him instantly famous when his design was chosen out of 744 architects for the design of Opera House Bastille in Paris. For Carlos this was a major breakthrough. He was hand-picked by French President Francois Mitterrand as the winner. In order to carry out the supervision of this prestigious project, Carlos moved to Paris and formed a team; it in turn gave him international recognition and opened doors to many countries, in addition to the fact that the Bastille Opera House attracts 900,000 spectators every year. His next accomplishment followed soon by winning the competition for an extremely advanced hospital in Weimar Germany as well as several competitions in the United Emirates such as the Sheikh Zayed Road Development Project (Abu Dhabi). That was followed by The National Bank of Abu Dhabi Headquarters, and Abu Dhabi Etisalat Telecom Administration Building; He was then asked for advice on Baniyas Road Development in Dubai, as well as the new Dubai Creek Hilton Hotel. In 1993 he set his sites on other projects in Europe such as the Salle des Spectacles in Mont-de-Marsan France, and the Thomson Headquarters Building Offices and Laboratories in Geneva. In 1992 he had returned to Uruguay and completed the International Airport of Laguna del Sauce (Punta del Este), in Uruguay. Then he participated in the competition for the Jiang Su Opera House in Nanjing China, where he obtained first prize; this was followed by other China projects. Ott continues to travel the world working on projects in America, Canada, Argentina, Chili, Peru and many Central, and South American, projects.

William Penn (494)

William Penn was born 14 Oct. 1644 in London; son of Admiral Sir William Penn and Margaret Jasper from the Netherlands. Young William grew up during the rule of Oliver Cromwell who led a Puritan rebellion against King Charles I, who was beheaded when Penn was three years old; his father was often at sea. Little William caught smallpox at a young age, lost his hair, and wore a wig until he left college. The family lived in the country, giving William a love for horticulture. He was educated mostly by private tutors and later at Christ Church, Oxford. There were no state schools all education was done by the Anglican Church, and it was expensive. Children from poor families needed a wealthy sponsor. Penn's education leaned heavily on the classical authors no modern writers including William Shakespeare were allowed. Foot racing was his favorite sport; he ran three miles to his tutors every day. The Anglican school was, strict, humorless and somber; teachers had to be pillars of virtue. He later opposed Anglicanism but had absorbed many puritan customs. He was known for his serious behavior and lack of humor. Admiral Penn and his family were exiled to Ireland. When Penn was 15, he met Quaker Thomas Loe, who was maligned by Catholics and Protestants; Loe was admitted to the Penn household. After Cromwell died, the Penn family returned to England and the middle class aligned themselves with Admiral Penn on a mission to bring back exiled Prince Charles. For his role in restoring the monarchy Admiral Penn was knighted and gained a powerful position. At age 18 young Penn was sent to Paris, and two years later he returned as a mature well mannered sophisticated gentleman, at a time London was in the grip of the 1665 plague, which killed about 100,000 people. (*Several centuries earlier Europe had been hit by the black (Bubonic) plague killing 200, million people almost 1/3rd of Europe*). Another major issue was the Fire of London that raged through the inner city, and burned for 4 days during September 1666. Young Penn converted to be a Quaker, which enraged his father, but young William was determined, and his father kicked him out; he then lived with Quaker families who were strict, refused to bow to superiors, believing all men were equal under God. Quakers refused to swear oaths to the king. Penn was close friends with George Fox the founder of Quakers. A lot of new sects popped up such as Behmenists, Seventh day Baptists, Soul Sleepers, Adamites, and many more. The Crown relentlessly persecuted all who were disloyal to Anglicanism. Penn was expelled from Oxford even though he had a famous father, he was jailed for his religious views, he oversaw the establishment of Pennsylvania as an advocate of religious freedom; he died at age 73, on July 30, 1718 in England.

Naftali Bennett (495)

Naftali Bennett was born 25 March, 1972 in Haifa Israel, the youngest of three sons born to Jim and Myrna Bennett, American-Jewish immigrants who moved back to Israel after living in the United States in July 1967. When Bennett was in 2nd grade the family moved to New Jersey, Both his parents were Jewish backgrounds from Ashkenazi. His father's ancestors were from Poland, Germany and the Netherlands. The family returned to Haifa when he was ten. In high school he was a youth leader. With the outbreak of the Yom Kippur War in October 1973, his father Jim Bennett returned to Israel to fight in the Israeli Defense Forces. Following that war, the rest of the family returned to Israel. In 1990 Bennett was drafted to serve in the elite Sayeret Metkal Commando unit, and after his regular service he was selected for officers training and became commander in the Maglan unit. In 2006 he entered politics serving as chief of staff for Benjamin Netanyahu until 2008. In 2011, together with Ayelet Shaked he co-founded the My Israel extra-parliamentary movement. In 2012 Bennett was elected as the party leader of the Jewish Home, under his leadership the party won 12 seats out of 120. He served under Prime Minister Netanyahu as minister of Economy mad Religious Services from 2013 to 2015. He was appointed Minister of Education in 2015; in December 2018 he defected from The Jewish Home to form the New Right. He had lost, but later regained his seat in the September 2019 Knesset election and was appointed Minister of Defense; in 2020 he succeeded Shaked to become the leader of Yamina alliance. On 2 June 2021 Bennett agreed to a rotation government with Yair Lapid, whereby Bennett would serve as Israel's Prime Minister until 2023, after which Lapid would assume the role until 2025. Bennett was sworn in on 13 June 2021, he believes in less government regulation of the private sector; he strongly believes and governs based on the principles that private businesses are the engine of economic growth. He favors social support of vulnerable populations such as elderly and disabled. He believes Israel needs to break the monopoly of the (much too powerful) tycoons of major labor unions, which in his opinions are strangling the economy; he implemented reforms to lower Israel's high food prices; import duties and barriers were reduced and mechanisms were set up to ensure more competition in Israeli food industry. He is married to Gilat a professional pastry chef; the couple has four children. Their eldest son Yonatan is named after Yonatan Netanyahu, and their youngest son David Emmanuel is named after Emmanuel Moreno, who was a comrade of Bennett in the Special Forces. The family adheres to Modern Orthodox Judaism and live 20 km (12 miles north of Tel Aviv)

Willard Metcalf (496)

Willard Metcalf was born July 1, 1858 in Lowell Massachusetts in a working-class family. He studied at the *Museum School of Fine Arts* in Boston, and later attended *Academie Julian* in Paris; he began painting in 1874, and became prominent as a landscape painter. In 1883 he left for Europe and stayed there till 1888, he studied in Paris with Gustave Boulanger and Jules Joseph Lefebvre. In the winter of 1884, he met John Twachtman in Paris and painted at Grez-sur-Loing alongside other American artists, such as Theodore Robinson. Traveling in those days was primarily by horse-drawn carriages, roadways were not plentiful and people often followed waterways to get to their destination. He traveled and painted till 1888, and returned to America and lived briefly in Boston, later had a solo exhibition in New York. In 1897 he was one of the ten American painters who seceded from the society of American artists, protesting the interest was too much in business and profit, and very little in art. For some years he was an instructor in the Women's Art School Cooper Union New York, and in the Art Students League New York. In 1893 he became a member of the American Watercolor Society in New York, and is generally associated with American impressionism, especially his paintings of Landscapes in the New England area as well as his involvement with the Old Lyme Art Colony at Old Lyme Connecticut; his most influential years likely were at the Cornish Art Colony. In 1899 Metcalf joined his friends Robert Reid and Edward Simmons in painting murals for a New York Courthouse, commissioned by a tobacco company. In preparation for a mural, he traveled to Havana Cuba in 1902 to make painted studies. That year he produced a series of notable landscapes including: *The boat landing* and *Battery Park-Spring*. These works were characterized by a new freshness. In 1904 he resided and painted steadily in Clark's Cove Maine. In 1907 *May Night* won the Corcoran Gallery of Art's gold medal, he was honored with the top purchase prize of $3.000; it became the first contemporary American painting to be bought by that institution. He frequently visited the Cornish Art Colony in New Hampshire returning there for many winters. He was good friends with Colonist Charles Platt, on whose Cornish Estate he honeymooned with his second wife, a great beginning but like all good things, they come to an end. His family strife did not improve, and in 1920 he and Henrietta divorced which spurred a period of drinking and a dramatic decrease in productivity; however, he rebounded and painted for a number of years in Vermont. In 1925, during a large exhibition, he died at age 66 on March 9, 1925 in New York City. At the time of his death, he had established himself as one of the great artists in Europe and in America.

Olga of Kiev also called Helga (497)

Olga was born about 890 was the first recorded female ruler in Russia and the first member of the ruling family of Kiev to adopt Christianity. She was the widow of Igor I, prince of Kiev, who was assassinated in 945 by his subjects. Because Igor's son Svyatoslav was still a minor, only three years old and too young to rule, Olga became Regent of the grand principality of Kiev from 945 to 964. The Drevlians who had murdered her husband came back and proposed that she marry her husband's murderer, Prince Mal. She decided, now that she replaced him as new ruler, instead of a marriage, one of her first official action was to have Igor's murderers executed; then adopt Orthodox Christianity made sure it become public knowledge, to do that she was first of the princely Kievan to be baptized about 957 at Constantinople, (now Istanbul). After her baptism she took the name Elena. Her Christian efforts were resisted by her son when he discovered what his mother had done, but were fully embraced by her grandson, Vladimir. She made great efforts to spread Christianity and convert the entire nation. Her exact birth-date is not known, it could be as early as 890 or as late as 925 AD. She was probably of Varangian origin, (*a name given by Greeks to Vikings thought to be Swedes*), and was most likely born in Pleskov. Little is known about her life before she was married to Igor I of Kiev, and the birth of their first son Sviatoslav. According to historian Alexey Karpov, Olga might have been about age 15 at the time of her marriage to Igor who was the son *and heir* of Rurik, founder of the Rurik dynasty. After his father died Igor had consolidated power in the region, conquering neighboring tribes and established Kiev as the capital. This federation became known as Kievan Rus, covering part of what is now known as Russia, Ukraine, and Belarus. According to Byzantine Chronicler Leo the Deacon, Igor's death was caused by a gruesome act of torture in which he was captured, tied to tree trunks and torn in two. Igor's son was three, making Olga the ruler on his behalf. Later her son disapproved of his mother's Christian conversion although he consented too many of her wishes. At the time of her death, Olga's attempt to make Kievan-Rus a Christian territory had been a failure; nonetheless her grandson Vladimir officially adopted Christianity in 988, therefore some of her efforts in that respect can be looked upon as a success in fulfilling the desires of his grandmother. Olga died 11 July 969 and was buried in Kiev. In 1547 (nearly 600 years after her death), the Russian Orthodox Church named Olga a saint. She was venerated as saint in all East Slavic speaking countries where churches use the Byzantine Rite, the Greek Catholic Church and the Roman Catholic Church and others all venerated Olga as saint.

Yulia Tymoshenko (498)

Yulia Tymoshenko Hrihyan was born on 27 November, 1960 in SSR Dnipropetrovsk, Ukraine, which was at that time part of the Soviet Union. Her mother Lyudmila was Ukranian and her Father Volodymir was Latvian. He abandoned his wife and Yulia when she was three years old; perhaps she was destined to enter the world without a father and be an independent lady. Yulia graduated from high school in 1978, then enrolled in Automatization and Telemechanics Department of the Dnepro University of Technology Mining Institute. In 1979 she transferred to the Economics classes of the Dnipropetrovsk State University majoring in cybernetic engineering, graduating in 1984 with first degree honors as an engineer-economist. In 1999, she defended her PhD dissertation titled State Regulation of the tax system at the Kyiv National Economic University. She was a successful Economist and Academic and from 1991 to 1995 she worked as general director of United Energy Systems; she reorganized the entire company and became president of the United Energy Systems of Ukraine. Under her management UESU successfully solved significant economic problem handling Ukraine's multi-billion debt for Russian natural gas making sure it was paid; Ukraine resumed international cooperation in machine building, the pipe industry and construction, and Ukraine's export of goods to Russia doubled; she put her stamp on the business world. At that time Tymoshenko was one of the richest people in Ukraine. (Just a personal observation here: after several years in business, she became wealthy, (quite opposite from America, here people become wealthy after being a politician for a few years; just an observation, I could be wrong). In 1996 she entered politics and was elected to the Ukranian Parliament winning a record 92.3% of the vote. As deputy prime minister she opposed President Leonid Kuchma, claiming that he was building a totalitarian system. From 2007 to 2010 she was elected the first woman prime minister of Ukraine, as well as the first woman to hold this post in the CIS countries, (*Central and Eastern Europe and the Commonwealth of Independent States*). She is the leader of the Batkivshchyna political party, and opposed membership of Ukraine in the Russian led Eurasian Customs Union, but supported NATO membership for Ukraine. She co-led the Orange Revolution, which was to protest giving President Victor Yanukovych to serve another term which resulted in her becoming a political prisoner, but after three years in jail she was released. From a sheer business perspective, she has been one of the most prominent figures in the history of Ukraine. In 2014 she finished second again losing to Petro Poroshenko. In the 2010, 2014 she had lost however in 2019 she was elected to lead her party and served as 10th and 13th Prime Minister of Ukraine.

Niuta Teitelbaum (499)

Niuta Teitelbaum was born 1917 in Poland and grew up in World War 2, became known as; *Little Wanda with the braids* and was one of the earliest, and youngest, volunteers to join the Jewish resistance movement in Warsaw Poland. She was one of the most perfect persons to be a member for their organization. A petite twenty-four-year-old looking only about sixteen, disguising her role dressed up as a Polish peasant that looked like *any* innocent little girl, you would never dislike, or *not* trust; but in reality, was *an assassin with a mission*. The German soldiers occupied Poland, and during that war little Wanda worked as a courier for Jewish Combat Organization and the Communist Gwardia Ludowa, (*the Polish Jewish Resistance movement*). With that innocent "*little girl look*", she could pass the guard of any home or business office and gain entrance while she carried a concealed weapon, that had been fitted with a silencer, and was trained well and knew how to use it. During the entire war she understood clearly what her real role in life was, it was being a *Nazi killer*, disguised as a little Polish peasant girl. She parlayed her innocent look to gain entrance to any Gestapo headquarters and was able to reach the ranking SS officer while sitting at his desk, the guards would never search her for weapons. She was able to gain safe entrance to any Gestapo headquarters, then silently shot the top-ranking officer and exit the building safely. One of Niuta's quotes was: "I am a Jew; my place is in the struggle against the Nazis for the honor of my people and for a free Poland." In the early days she strolled up to the guards at the Nazi headquarters dressed as a Polish farm girl and with her most innocent look she asked to see her "*boyfriend*" who was the highest-ranking officer in the building, naming him by his name. She looked pregnant and said her visit was on a personal matter. Guards let her in and gave her the "*boyfriend's*" room number. She walked in, found him sitting at his desk dressed in his black SS uniform, walked in pulled her gun with silencer shot him in the head and walked out of the building smiling at the guards who opened the doors for her. Another time she killed two Gestapo agents and wounded a third. The third was taken to the hospital; she followed him, disguised herself as a doctor, was able to get access to his room, then shot and killed him including the person who guarded him. Niuta avoided capture for nearly 3 years, but in 1943, two months after the Warsaw Ghetto uprising the Gestapo burst into her room, she was captured, severely tortured and executed at age twenty-five. To the Germans, she was little Wanda with the braids, but to the Polish underground she was known as the Heroine of Warsaw. It is my understanding there are books written about her life, but I was not able to find more about Niuta in public records then reported here.

Jack Webb (500)

John Randolph Webb was born April 2, 1920 in Santa Monica California. His father left home before he was born; therefore, Webb never knew him nor did he ever see him. He grew up in the Bunker Hill section of Los Angeles; in the late 1920's and early 1930's he lived in the parish of Our Lady of Loretto Church, where he served as an altar boy and attended the elementary school in Echo Park. After that went to Belmont High School near downtown Los Angeles, and wrote in their student yearbook of 1938, "*You showed me magnificent warmth and friendship; I will carry with me forever*". Then went to St John's University Minnesota where he studied art. During World War II he enlisted in the United States Air Corps, but had to wash out of flight training, because he was given a hardship discharge due to the fact that he was the primary financial support for both his mother and grandmother. He was raised by his mother in dire poverty that preceded the depression. What is surprising about him is that he suffered from acute asthma from age six, and in that condition still smoked three packs of cigarettes a day. He moved to San Francisco and tried several radio shows, but they did not go well, he then turned to comedy but that did not do any better making Jack change to motion pictures for a while; after that he attempted Crime lab which did better and evolved into a TV show called Dragnet. In his vision for Dragnet, Webb said he intended to perform a service for the police, although his great love was movies and his dream was to direct them. He befriended an LAPD consultant and he tested a show called Dragnet on NBC beginning in February 1963, he had become head of production for Warner Bros Television of 77 Sunset Strip (1958) sending its rating into a death spiral resulting in Jack getting fired; coincidently they owned the rights to Dragnet and Webb was invited to a new Dragnet TV movie. That turned out well in industry previews and NBC and Universal persuaded him to do a new TV series which lasted three and a half seasons and went on to smash success as well as the syndicated reruns. Over the next five seasons he regularly blasted Marijuana, and LSD, the series popularity could have ensured its continuation indefinitely, but by then Webb had invented a new Dragnet and it succeeded well enough, it lasted three seasons; unbeknown to his fans he possessed a healthy sense of humor; this became evident at a guest appearance on the Tonight Show with Johnny Carson. On December 23 1982 (not unexpected) Jack Webb died of a massive heart attack, in West Hollywood at only 62 years of age. He left us the catchphrase "*Just the facts ma'am*", which he may, or may not have said; nevertheless, his fans, (of which I am one), have credited that phrase to him.

Kathy Sparks (501)

Kathy put the baby in bed then took her policemen husband's revolver to her head and heard a click; the gun jammed as she tried to put her empty life to an end and now even the gun failed her, she called her mother-in-law who lived three blocks away, who said: "Kathy put the gun away, pick up your baby and come here." Kathy did and a few minutes later she was sitting on her mother in law's porch who said: "Kathy you are trying to take your own life, why not give the Lord an opportunity to live His life through you." She thought, why not, I can't even kill myself, with or without the bullet her life seemed to be at an end and now even the gun has failed me. The night had begun with plans to end it all, instead a new era was beginning to dawn. Now 45 years later Kathy still marvels at the grace that found her on that terrible night, the first miracle was: The gun did not go off; the second was the depression that instantly left her, and the third they did not go through with the planned divorce. When Mike found out that Kathy had changed, he went ranting off to his mother who handed him a Bible and said: here read this: *Every answer to your problems is in that book*. Mike did, he read it from cover to cover and discovered a very different life. Kathy, instead of being depressed, went back to work cheerfully to the abortion clinic where she worked. She had immersed herself totally in the abortion issue and loved the professionalism of the abortionists, feeling good about helping. Her life was now near perfect, working in a medical clinic, where abortions were done six days a week, 40 a day. She listened as counselors convincing the uncertain young women persuading them to kill their babies. Seeing babies being flushed down the toilet she was helping to kill these babies. Mike was still reading through his Bible and one morning Kathy thought what I am doing here, I am helping to kill children, then someone grabbed her by the arm and said "Kathy pull yourself together," and began berating her. That night she had a bad dream and knew God gave her that dream and told the clinic director the next morning: I have become a Christian and this is my last day here, then walked out and left. Mike too had a major change, and told Kathy we are going to be involved in pregnancy center ministry. Soon after that, Kathy was on radio programs talking about her experience in the abortion clinic. In no time that ministry grew in to what is now known as *Mosaic Pregnancy and Health Centers*, headquartered in Granite City Illinois. Mike has passed away from cancer, now 34 years later Kathy and her team have served more the 20,000 clients, doing pregnancy testing, ultrasounds, helped counsel teenagers about sexually transmitted diseases, adoption referrals teach classes on parenting, but Cathy continues to live their dream, now operating a real health center, and even do post-abortion counseling.

Kim Potter (502)

Kim Potter on February 18, 2022 the judge ruled: 16 months in jail & 6 months supervised release. was born and raised in 1972 in Minnesota by her parents and as a child she always wanted to be a police officer and watched police movies since her childhood. She completed her college and went to the police academy where she was a brilliant student. Her parents supported her career choice. She married her boyfriend, Jeffrey; they have two sons who are 20 and 23 years old. A police traffic stop at one time would have been routine, but with the disrespect and anti police demonstrations, such a stop has become dangerous. She stopped Daunte Wright, at first for an expired registration and an illegal air freshener, while she ran a search report an open arrest warrant, was found. He was not cooperating with the police and Kim, who is a 26-year police veteran, decided to make an arrest. This resulted in a heated argument, and Wright drove off. (An experienced police officer only uses the gun when there is no other way, according to my brother who is a policeman). Kim decided to resort to the Taser gun, but in the heat of the moment she made a bad mistake and accidentally used a real bullet and Wright drove away for some distance and died, she was heard saying: "*I grabbed the wrong gun!*" She resigned from the police department a few days later. Kim Potter was prosecuted and given a jury trial. It was a case of a white police officer shooting and killing a black person. That issue alone is toxic. During the trial she testified that she had never used the Taser gun, nor ever fired a handgun while on duty; records show no complaints were ever filed against her in the entire 26 years that she served as a police officer. During the trial 30 people including Potter took the stand; then the case was given to the jury who deliberated about 27 hours. The maximum penalty for first degree manslaughter with a firearm could be as much as 15 years in prison. Since Potter has no criminal history, Minnesota sentencing guidelines might recommend between 6 and 8 years in prison. Judge Regina Chu thanked the jury, which midway through deliberations appeared to struggle to reach a consensus and said thank you for your sacrifices. Demonstrators carrying *Black Lives Matter* signs applauded when the verdict was read "*Guilty on all counts*", a brass band even played. It was a guilty verdict on first- and second-degree manslaughter; Potter was remorseful and her defense counsel asked the judge's permission for her to go home before sentencing. The judge denied that request she was handcuffed, escorted out of the courtroom, and transferred to the Minnesota correctional facility in Shakopee 25 miles southwest of Minneapolis. Sentencing has been set for Feb. 18, 2022. Why is Kim here? She served 26 years as a police officer in a city with a history of racial tension with a clean record, if God allowed no mistakes; none of us would live long.

Nigel Rowe (503)

Nigel Rowe and his wife Sally made a discovery that was rather new to them. Our parents turned us over to the teachers to be taught math, reading, geography, music, and speech and right and wrong to prepare us for an adult world. School questions were covered in class and at the dinner table at home. That was normal 80 years ago. What has changed? Nigel and Sally began to see disturbing changes in the children and contacted their Christian school to see if something might have happened at school, had they got in to arguments with other children? Was there a bully in the school? Or the curriculum was too complicated? May be the children needed to be at a lower grade? They were in a Christian School practicing religious principles comparable to the family faith, and to receive a Christian education is rather costly for a young family. One day a 6-year-old boy decided he wanted to identify and dress as a girl and wanted teachers and students to treat him as a girl. The boy was in the same class as one of Nigel and Sally's sons. The same scenario had happened with their eldest son, who also came home with strange questions: is it ok for a man to marry a man? Can boys become girls? It began to look like the school may have sold out to the SIECUS material, which is the result of Alfred Kinsey's perverted *pseudo* science, which was not science but perversion. The school taught one thing, and the parents were attempting to teach them the Biblical way, which confused the children; the parents noticed a change in their son's behavior. It became clear that their sons were indoctrinated with teaching that was anti-biblical, the school was promoting transgender ideology, the guidelines for the school were not written from a Christian perspective but had been drafted by LGBTQ activists and were aimed to embed transgender ideology, into the curriculum, with guidelines that were upheld by local authorities and the Department of Education. The head teacher of the Church of England said: <u>*accept it*</u>! As Bible-believing Christians, they could <u>*never*</u> do that; why sacrifice for a Christian education? They felt sure that there would be many parents in agreement with them, <u>that may have been so</u>, but none were willing to stand with them; they were told by professionals: "If a child wants to identify as the opposite sex, we just have to accept it." The couple has been working with "<u>*real*</u>" experts who explained the harmful impact of such teaching on the minds of young children. Why are Nigel and Sally Rowe on these pages? They took their children out of school and began home schooling and said: As Christians we are called to stand for truth, <u>if not us, who will</u>? Transgender perversion is not limited to England, but is clearly a ubiquitous evil monster that threatens the innocence of children on a world-wide scale,

Alex Newman (504)

Alex Newman is an award-winning international journalist, educator, author, and consultant who seeks to glorify God in everything he does. Since I changed my occupation and began writing these books, I have asked God: Please make me half as good as Alex Newman, he is a contributor to WND (World Net Daily) and has written for a wide array of publications here in the United States. I have seen his material in papers and publications abroad, in countries such as Switzerland and in New Zealand; His bio indicates that he has lived in eight countries including U.S. Mexico and a number of European nations and is quite fluent on economics as well as multiple languages. He is a frequent guest on national and international TV and radio programs and has been a weekly guest on the nationally syndicated Phyllis Schlafly Show and others including Michael Savage. He is married and they have four children. I may not have seen much of his material, but the best essay I ever saw was written in the _December 1-7, 2021 Epoch Times_ titled: The totalitarian Agenda behind LGBT Sex-Ed Revolution at School. In that commentary he points out the extreme sexualization and LBGBTQ-plus indoctrination of children at younger and younger ages in public schools that are now ubiquitous nationwide-and is part of an agenda that goes well beyond just encouraging confusion and promiscuity; the real goal of that agenda is to destroy the nuclear family as the foundation of civilization. It starts as early as kindergarten with children being introduced to homosexuality, gender fluidity and LGBT material now mandated under state law. Throughout elementary school, children are exposed to obscene images that have been widely condemned as pornographic in books such as "_it's perfectly normal_". Under 3Rs, by the time children are age 12-13 they are taught to rely on _Planned Parenthood_ for information and services. This indoctrination is in spite of the fact that the American College of Pediatricians argues it is "_child abuse_" for adults to convince children that a life of chemical and surgical impersonation of the opposite sex is normal or healthy. This material teaches the children aged 5 through 8 to _ignore_ their parents and impersonate the opposite sex if they feel they are born in the wrong body; numerous state education bureaucrats have endorsed these programs, 7th graders are taught that anal sex with condoms is a "_low risk_" activity. The Centers for Disease Control and Prevention found that condoms are only 60 to 70% effective in preventing HIV even with perfect and consistent use. The essay is long and detailed. In my opinion in his book _Crimes of the educators_: how Utopians are using Government Schools to destroy America's children. I can think of no one who has expressed it more succinct as Alex has, being one of the greatest journalists.

Renzo Piano (505)

Renzo Piano was born on 14 September 1937 in Genoa, Italy, a picturesque Italian city, experiencing sub-tropical Mediterranean climate. He was born and raised into a family of builders. His grandfather had created a masonry enterprise which was expended by his father and his father's three brothers into the firm Fratilli Piano. The firm constructed houses, factories, and construction materials. Renzo studied architecture at Milan Polytechnic University. He graduated in 1964 with a dissertation about modular coordination supervised by Giuseppe Ciribini and began working with experimental lightweight structures and basic shelters. Piano taught at the Polytechnic University from 1965 until 1968 and expended his horizons and technical skills by working in two large international firms for the modernist architect Louis Kahn in Philadelphia and for the Polish engineer Zygmunt Stanislaw Makowski in London. He completed his first building, the IPE factory in Genoa, in 1968 with a roof of steel and reinforced polyester and created a continuous membrane for the covering of a pavilion at the Milan Triennale in the same year. In 1970, he received his first international commission, for <u>the Pavilion of Italian industry for Expo 70</u> in Osaka, Japan. He collaborated with his brother Ermanno and the family firm, which manufactured the structure. It was lightweight and original composed of steel and reinforced polyester, and it appeared to be simultaneously artistic and industrial. The 1970 Osaka structure was greatly admired by the British architect Richard Rogers and in 1971 the two men decided to open their own firm, *Piano and Rogers*, where they worked together from 1971 to 1977. The first project of the firm was the administrative building of BandB Italia, an Italia furniture company, in Novedrate, Como, Italy. The design featured suspended container and an open bearing structure, with the conduits for heating and water on the exterior painted in bright colors (blue, red and yellow). These unusual features attracted considerable attention in the architectural world, and influenced the choice of the jurors who selected Piano and Rogers to design the Pompidou center. In 1971, the 34-year-old Piano and Richard Rogers 38, in collaboration with the Italian architect Gianfranco Franchini, competed with the major architectural firms in the United States and Europe and were awarded the commission for the most prestigious project in Paris the Centre George Pompidou, the new French national museum of 20th century art. He won the Pritzker architecture prize in 1998, Potsdamer Platz in Berlin, New York Times Building, Shard London Bridge, Astrup Fearnley Museum of Modern Art in Oslo, Centro de Arte Botin, Spain, the Nasher Sculpture center in Dallas Texas, Aurora Place Sydney. He has designed many unique buildings in many countries.

Tim Scott (506)

Tim Scott was born 19 September 1965 in North Charleston South Carolina U.S. son of Frances and Ben Scott Sr. His parents divorced when he was 7. He grew up in a working-class poverty with his mother who worked 16-hour days to support her family. His 2 brothers are serving in high positions in America's armed forces. Tim graduated from R B Stall High School and attended Presbyterian Collage from 1983 to 1984 on a football scholarship and graduated Charleston Southern University in 1988 with a Bachelor of Science in Political Science. He is an alumnus of South Carolina's Palmetto Boys State Program an experience he cites as influential in his decision to enter public service. For his career he ran an insurance agency for All State Insurance Company, proving that he understands the world of business, making him a successful politician. He ran in a February 1995 special election for the Charleston County Council at large seat that was vacated by Keith Summey who resigned after he was elected mayor of North Charleston. Scott won the seat as a Republican, receiving nearly 80% of the vote in a white-majority district. He became the first black Republican elected to any office in South Carolina since the late 19th century, and was re-elected to the County Council in 2000 winning in a white-majority district. In 2004 he was re-elected again with 61% of the vote, defeating Democrat Son of mayor Summey. Scott served on the council from 1995 until 2008, becoming chairman in 2007. In 1997 he posted the Ten Commandments outside the Council chambers, saying it would remind members of the absolute rules they should follow. The county council unanimously approved the display, and Scott nailed the King James Version of the Ten Commandments to the wall. As expected, it did not take long before the ACLU and Americans United for Separation of Church and State challenged this in a federal suit. After an initial court ruling that the display was unconstitutional the council settled out of court to avoid accruing more legal fees. Scott said about the costs of the suit it was worth it. In 2010 Scott entered election for lieutenant governor, but switched to run for South Carolina's 1st Congressional district after Harry Brown announced his retirement. The first district is partially based in Charleston. Scott finished 1st in the nine-candidate race, June 8 Republican primary receiving a plurality of 32% of the vote, in the runoff he was endorsed by the Cub for growth, Tea Party groups, Sarah Palin, Eric Cantor, Mike Huckabee and South Carolina senator Jim de Mint. With all that support, he defeated his opponent Paul Thurmond in a 68% to 32% and won every county in the district. Tim Scott is now serving as United States Senator from South Carolina and has retained that seat since January 2, 2013.

Pete Hegseth (507)

Peter Brian Hegseth was born June 6, 1980 in Forest Lake Minnesota US and attended Forest Lake high school there; after that he graduated from Princeton University with a BA, while he was there, he was the publisher of *The Princeton Tory* (a conservative student-run publication.) And Harvard University with an MPP, (*Masters of Public Policy*). He served in the Minnesota Army National Guard in the Iraq war and the war in Afghanistan; he was executive director of Political Advocacy groups Vets for Freedom and Concerned Veterans for America. He was considered to lead the United States Department of Veterans affairs in the Trump Administration, but major veterans groups objected to the potential pick. In January 2017, David Shulkin was selected instead. Hegseth has been active in conservative and Republican politics since his days as an undergraduate at Princeton University. In 2016, he emerged as a strong supporter of Donald Trump's presidential candidacy and served as an occasional advisor throughout his presidency. Hegseth reportedly persuaded Trump to pardon the three American soldiers accused, or convicted, of war crimes related to the shooting of non-combatants in Iraq. He has provoked controversy and criticism for his role in this regard. Hegseth, who was a platoon leader at Guantanamo Bay during his military service, has also controversially defended the treatment of detainees there. In July 2019, he said that one of the Muslim members of Congress, Rashid Tlaib, has a Hamas agenda; In that same year he lamented that young kids voting are worried about the adverse effects of climate change, and criticized universities for teaching students about environmentalism and *radical environmentalism* rather than the real threat such as Islamic extremism. In 2020 he expressed strong support of President Trump's decision to kill Iranian General Qasum Soleimani; he also called on Trump to bomb the Iranian homeland, including cultural sites in Iran if they were storing weapons. He has been a regular guest on *Unfiltered* with Dan Bongino since 2021. He wrote the foreword to the 2017 book *the case against the establishment* by Nick Adams and Dave Erickson. He returned to active duty in 2012, and was deployed to Afghanistan with the Minnesota Army National Guard acting as a senior counterinsurgency at the training center in Kabul; Hegseth a Major, currently serves in the individual ready reserve. He has been awarded two Bronze Stars for his service overseas. He worked briefly at the Manhattan Institute for Policy Research. He ran for the Republican nomination For the US Senate seat in Minnesota, in 2012, but withdrew from the race in May 2012. After that in 2014 he joined Fox News as a contributor. Pete Hegseth legacy is that he has been a strong supporter of Veterans affairs.

Anselm of Canterbury (508)

Anselm of Canterbury, (also called) Anselmo d'Aosta named after his birthplace, Anselm of Bec was born in about in the year 1033 in the Roman Empire in Aosta Kingdom of Burgundy, now Italy, Aosta remained part of the post-Carolingian kingdom of Burgundy until the death of Rudolf III in 1032 The Emperor and the count of Blois then went to war over his succession. Humbert the Whitehanded count of Maurien, so distinguished himself, he was granted a new county carved out of Aosta. Anselm was a Benedictine monk, abbot, philosopher, and theologian, who held the office of Archbishop of Canterbury from 1093 to 1109. As archbishop, he defended the church's interests in England amid the Investiture Controversy. *(also called Conflict, was a Church/State issue in medieval Europe about the right to choose Bishops, and Abbots of monasteries as well as the pope until the Holy Roman Emperors renounced the right to choose the Pope, leaving it to the church, although the conflict lasted 46 years and was resolved in 1122.)* As archbishop, he defended the church's interest in England. For his resistance to the English kings William II and Henry I, he was exiled twice; in exile he helped guide the Greek Bishops of Southern Italy to adopt Roman rights at the council of Bari. He worked for the primacy of Canterbury over the Bishops of York and Wales and at his death he appeared to have been successful, Pope Paschal II later reversed himself and restored York's independence. Anselm is believed to have been the most noted theologian of all times, his books representing the spiritual independence of the church. Beginning at Bec, Anselm composed dialogues and treatises with rational and philosophical approach, sometimes causing him to be credited as the founder of Scholasticism. Despite his lack of recognition in this field in his own time, Anselm is now famed as the originator of the ontological argument for the existence of God and of the satisfaction theory of atonement. He was proclaimed a Doctor of the Church by a bull of Pope Clement XI in 1720. His works were copied and disseminated in his lifetime; he influenced scholars such as Bonaventure, Thomas Aquinas, William of Ockham and more. His thoughts have guided much discussion on the procession of the Holy Sprit and the atonement; as well as controversies over free will and predestination. Anselm has been called the most luminous and penetrating intellect between Augustine and Thomas Aquinas. He and the thinkers who followed him were among the most brilliant periods of Western philosophy, innovating logic, semantics, ethics, metaphysics, and other areas of philosophical theology. He died 21 April 1109 in Canterbury England, and was canonized by the church as a saint.

Immanuel Kant (509)

Immanuel Kant was born 22 April 1724 in Konigsberg, Kingdom of Prussia, and (now Russia). He was a German philosopher and one of the central Enlightenment thinkers. Kant's comprehensive and systematic works in epistemology, metaphysics, ethics and aesthetics have made him one of the most influential figures in modern Western philosophy. In his doctrine of transcendental idealism, Kant argued that space and time are mere forms of intuition which structure all experience, and therefore that while "things-in-themselves" exist and contribute to experience; they are nonetheless distinct from the objects of experience. From this it follows that the objects of experience are mere "appearances", and that the nature of things as they are in themselves, is consequently unknowable to us. In an attempt to counter the skepticism, he found in the writings of David Hume, (1711-1776), he wrote _the Critique of Pure Reason_ (1781), (one of his most well-known works; in there Kant is credited with one of the cornerstones of Western Philosophy). He published a second edition of _the Critique of Pure Reason_ in (1787). Kant believed that reason is also the source of morality; he was an exponent of the idea that perpetual peace could be secured through universal democracy and international cooperation. According to Associate Professor M. Rohlf, (historian of modern philosophy who specializes in Kant), said this about Kant: He believes that every human being is endowed with a conscience. In some areas Kant is concise, but the nature of Kant's religious views continues to be the subject of scholarly dispute, with viewpoints ranging from the impression that he shifted from an early defense of an ontological argument of the existence of God, to a principled agnosticism; Nietzsche, claimed that Kant had "theologian blood" and was merely a sophisticated apologist for traditional Christian faith. Kant's moral philosophy is a philosophy of freedom... Kant believed that if a person could not act otherwise, then his or her act can not have a moral worth. Further he believed that every human being is endowed with a conscience that makes him or her aware that the moral law has authority over them. We could likely fill several books if we expend much further on Kant's works. Kant has been criticized for his racism presented in some of his lesser-known papers, such as "_On the Use of Theological Principles in Philosophy_" and on _the Different Races of Man_". Although he was a proponent of scientific racism for much of his career, Kant's views on race changed significantly in the last decade of his life, when he rejected racial hierarchies and European colonialism; On 12 February 1804 at age 79 Immanuel Kant died in East Prussia. He is generally considered one of the most profound and original philosophers who ever lived,

Henry L. Deneen (510)

Since my partner of more than 50 years, Hal Jones, died of a heart attack on October 27, 2020; (Hal and his brother Lloyd were high scholars when they came after school to clean my financial office, we developed a very close friendship that resulted in managing some political campaigns and Hal's father invited us to every family gathering, even adopted us as part of the Jones family. It seemed like Hal was *"tailor made"* for what he did and we believed that he really was irreplaceable. As board chairman we often talked about it but thought Hal is young and there is ample time to plan for that. When Hal died, I asked God*; Shall we, or shall we not, continue*? Thanks to Lana (Hal's wife who traveled everywhere with him), she was not prepared to abandon the work they had begun together with the blessings of Dr Bill Bright. Since I am only a few years away from age 90, Ed Sauer stepped in my shoes as board chairman and has done an amazing job. A search committee was organized who began looking for a qualified person that could step in Hal's shoes and carry on the work of GHNI (Global Hope Network International), certainly not an easy task to find a person that can communicate, is able to fly from country to country, *and* upon arrival hit the ground running. The committee found a candidate and in light of the fact that board members are scattered across the Globe, Henry Deneen and his bride Celia were presented to us by the modern technology of *Zoom* (such a meeting is far above my pay-grade), however in my opinion *we may have hit the jackpot*. Henry and Celia have been married for 35 years and are the parents of four grown and supportive children. He will serve as executive director and comes with 30 years of experience in leadership for international and cross-cultural work, most recently as an attorney and Director for Leadership Development at Murphy and Grantland, P.A. in Columbia South Carolina and as Co-Founder and Executive Director of the Center of Global Strategies. Prior to that, the family lived in France working as strategy leader in North Africa, to connect professionals in the West with business and government leaders in isolated countries. His work has created broader efforts for development initiatives in Libya, Sudan, Yemen, Turkmenistan, Myanmar, Bulgaria, Dubai, Vietnam and others. He also served in South Carolina as a mediator and attorney, a Municipal judge, and as chief legal Counsel for the Governor of South Carolina. He has an earned Doctorate in Executive Leadership with a focus on emotional intelligence. His focus is on connecting people and nations; Henry leads the Litigation Defense College at MandG, welcoming young attorneys providing them with training and mentors these young people for the first 3 years of their practice. His wife Celia is a Licensed Professional Counselor.

Serena Williams (511)

Serena Jameka Williams was born September 26, 1981 in Saginaw Michigan US to Oracene Price and Richard Williams; she was the youngest of five sisters and has seven more half siblings. Serena was home schooled by her father, as a small child the family lived in Compton California, and there she began to love tennis and was coached by her parents. At her age 9 the family moved to Florida and Serena attended the tennis academy of Rick Macci who began coaching Serena although he respected her father, but did not always agree on his coaching style. When she was ten, he wanted her to go slow on tennis and focuses more on school work. Some of that was driven by racism; he had heard white parents talk about the Williams sisters in a derogatory manner during tournaments. Williams is 5 ft 9 and is an aggressive baseliner, whose game is centered on her powerful serve and forceful ground-strokes. She became professional and won 23 Grand Slam singles titles, the most by any player in the Open Era, and the second most of all time behind Margaret Court. The Women's Tennis Association (WTA) ranked her singles world No.1 on eight separate occasions; on her 6th occasion she held the ranking for 186 consecutive weeks, in total she has been WTA No 1 for 319 weeks. She is the only American player to win more than 20 majors; Serena is widely regarded to be one of the greatest women tennis players of all time. She holds the most major titles in singles, doubles and mixed doubles. She has won a record 13 Grand Slam singles titles on hard court. She and her sister Venus have won 14 Grand Slam doubles titles. Serena got married after a one year courtship to Reddit co-founder of Alexis Ohanian on November 16, 2017, they met in Rome, and in September 2017 Serena gave birth to her daughter Alexis Olympia. Serena was raised Jehovah's Witness, but she has never practiced it. After giving birth she suffered a pulmonary embolism, and was devastated about it, leaving her bedridden for six weeks. In August 2018 she revealed she was suffering from postpartum depression. In the early 2000's, Williams signed a five-year endorsement deal with Nike in 2004 for $40 million and has been endorsed by the company for clothing apparel and footwear ever since, Nike designs custom clothing for Williams which she wears on the court along with custom footwear. There seems to be no question about it, but Serena Williams has been hailed by many coaches, players, sportscasters to be one of the best female tennis players some have called her the greatest tennis player ever. She has been a positive influence on young girls and boys who see Williams as a role model and an ambassador of tennis. Some have called her the best player of all times. On December 29, 2019, the Associated Press named Serena Williams Female Athlete of the Decade for the 2010s.

Joseph John Gurney (512)

Joseph John Gurney was born 2 August 1788 in Earlham Hall, Norfolk, England, the 10th child of John Gurney of Gurney's Bank; he was the brother of Samuel Gurney a prison and social reformer, his friends were anti-slavery campaigners. He was educated by a private tutor at Oxford; all were members of non-conformist religious groups and were ineligible to matriculate at the English universities. (*In those days of English Church history, it was generally understood that such a person would be a Protestant and refused to subscribe to the teachings of the Church of England*), In 1817 he joined his sister Elizabeth Fry in her attempt to end capital punishment, and institute improvements in prisons. They talked with several members of Parliament but had little success. Gurney was a recorded Quaker minister, (*this means he was noted as a person gifted by God for preaching and teaching*), even though Quakers did not designate individuals to take substantial roles in their worship, nor financially supported its ministers unless their travels in that role otherwise would have been impractical. Gurney and Fry visited prisons all over Great Britain to gather evidence of the horrible conditions in them to present to Parliament. They published their findings in a book entitled *Prisons in Scotland and the North of England*. Eventually Robert Peel, the Home Secretary, took an interest in prison-reform and introduced *the Goals Act 1823*, which called for salaries to wardens, (rather than their being supported by prisoners themselves), and putting female wardens in charge of female prisoners. He also prohibited the use of irons or manacles. Gurney campaigned against slavery during trips to North America and the West Indies from 1837-1840. He also promoted the Friends' belief and world peace in Ireland Scotland, the Netherlands, Belgium, Germany and Denmark, as well as promoting the abolition of Capital Punishment. He advocated total abstinence from alcohol and wrote a tract titled "*Water is best*". He caused a serious controversy among Quakers when he stressed the traditional Protestant belief that salvation is through faith in Christ, his followers were called Gurneyite Quakers. By 1820 his friend Wilberforce had turned 60 and was in unreliable health, yet his mental strength was scarcely impaired and his awareness of what remained to be done to put an end to negro-slavery, the cause to which he had dedicated his life for over 30 years drove him on. His dear friend John Joseph Gurney ministered to Wilberforce till his death at age 73, both men were able to witness the total abolition act of slavery, which passed in 1833. Wilberforce passed 3 days later and John Joseph Gurney died at age 58 on 4 January 1847, leaving a legacy of being a dedicated Quaker his entire life, and not abandoning his dear friend William Wilberforce during his final days.

Elizabeth Fry (513)

Elizabeth Fry was born 21 May 1780 in Gurney Court in Norwich England and is sometimes referred to as Betsy Fry and is part of a prominent Quaker family, the Gurneys. Her childhood family home was Earlham Hall, which is now part of the University of East Anglia. Her father John Gurney was a partner in Gurney Bank. Her mother Catherine was a member of the Barclay family who were among the founders of Barclays Bank; her mother died when she was 12 years old. As one of the oldest girls in the family, Elizabeth was partly responsible for the care and education of the younger children, including her brother Joseph John Gurney, (who became a philanthropist, later ministering to such people as William Wilberforce). One of her sisters was a writer on education. According to Elizabeth's diary, she was moved by the preaching of Priscilla Hanna Gurney, and several others. She met Joseph Fry, when she was 20 years old, a banker and a cousin of the Bristol Fry family who was a Quaker, and was also interested in Prison reform. They married 19 August 1800 in Norwich and moved to London, there had 11 children, 5 sons and 6 daughters. Elizabeth helped the homeless, establishing a nightly shelter after seeing the body of a young boy in the winter of 1819. One of her admirers was Queen Victoria who granted her an audience a few times and contributed money to her cause. Another admirer was Robert Peel who passed several acts in Parliament to further her cause, including _the Goals Act 1823,_ although it was not effective because there were no inspectors to make sure the act was being followed. She became the major driving force behind new legislation to improve treatment of prisoners, especially female inmates, and as such she acquired the name "_Angel of Prisons_" She kept extensive diaries where she was explicit with protecting female prisoners from rape and sexual exploitation. In addition to her support of Queen Victoria, she was supported in her efforts by both Emperor Alexander I and Emperor Nicholas I of Russia and was in correspondence with both, as well as their wives and the Empress Mother. Elizabeth Fry died from a stroke on 12 October 1845. In her memory the first Elizabeth Fry Women's shelter opened its door in 1849. Due to her work as a prison reformer, there are many memorials, shelter homes, buildings, and plaques and organizations throughout England and Canada. Elizabeth visited 106 transport ships and saw 12,000 prisoners and asked authorities to support her work, she stayed overnight in some prisons and asked authorities to come and see for themselves what conditions prisoners were forced to live in. In commemoration of her achievements, she was depicted on the _Bank of England Five Pound note_ circulating 2002 to 2016.

Rachel Campos-Duffy (514)

Rachel Campos-Duffy was born Oct. 22, 1971 in Arizona US, to Miguel Campos and Maria del Pillar, junior –high school teachers in Chandler Arizona. She and her siblings were raised in a strict Catholic home. Campos-Duffy graduated from Seton Catholic Preparatory High School. Her grandparents immigrated to the US from Mexico. She graduated from Arizona State University in 1993, with a degree in economics, and was awarded the Woodrow Wilson Graduate Fellowship, which she had planned to use and become a college professor. Campos earned a masters degree in international affairs from the University of California. She was cast on *The Real World: San Francisco* in January 1994, and lived in the house on Russian Hill in SF with her 6 housemates from Feb. to Jun. The season premiered on July 6, 1994. After her stint on *The Real World*, she was involved in a head-on car-collision where the driver of the oncoming vehicle fell asleep at the wheel. Her boyfriend, and his friend who was driving, died; Campos was thrown out of the vehicle and was seriously injured causing long-term injuries to her right leg. She married her All-Stars Co-star Sean Duffy. They lived in Ashland Wisconsin, where Duffy was the District Attorney. In 2008 Campos-Duffy revealed that she suffered 2 miscarriages. In 2019 their ninth child was born, a little girl with Down syndrome; her husband, (who was serving in Congress), resigned his position to focus more time and attention on his family. She was talented and tried for a spot on The View, but was not selected. Rachel is a published author, television personality, communications consultant, specializing in political analysis and parenting. She is the host of America's # 1 rated cable news morning show *Fox and Friends* on the Fox News Network; she has also appeared as a frequent guest on NBC's *Today show* and ABC's *The View*. In 2008 she co-hosted the series *Speaking of Women's Health* on the Lifetime Network with the legendary Florence Henderson. When she was asked: Why nine kids? She responded: I did not have a number in mind, we didn't plan any, they just kind of happened. I've taken each one as a blessing sent to me by God. The best compliment I have gotten is from teachers who say they can tell that my kids come from a big family because they can see, and anticipate, other people's needs and do not think the world revolves around them. They have to help; there is a lot of cooperation and teamwork that happens in a big family... I am the oldest in my family and my husband was the tenth of eleven, faith is very important in a big family. Why is she here? She is a great newscaster, successful wife and mother of 9 children; I am one of seven, as well as parent and foster parent of 7 (including 5 foster boys). Rachel demonstrates a commitment to the welfare of our nation's youth.

Pete Anderson (515)

After Pete graduated from Westminster Seminary, he and his wife Martha moved to Hawaii and founded Trinity Presbyterian Church in Kailua and an additional church in Mililani, and Kapolei. I was working in the business world of finance and gave motivation speeches, and befriended Pete and had frequent lunch meetings with him, instead of me motivating Pete, he motivated me and often told me his goals were not limited to Hawaii, but on the 1, 3 billion people in the continent of Africa. Pete made more than 50 trips there and with the help of his brother Syd they formed Trinity Center for World Mission (TCWM) and intended to reach every person on the African Continent; to do that, they would be training new generations of those who could teach and equip ministers. For a greater impact they started radio stations. Pete drafted a letter titled "<u>Dream the Impossible Dream</u>"; in there he expresses this motto; Expect great things <u>from</u> God and attempt great things <u>for</u> God. TCWM believes that God can do more than we ask, think, or imagine. He can change the human heart; we dared to dream the impossible dream. This dream is now coming true; God has risen up TCWM and a host of partners to train a new generation of pastors and Christian leaders in Central Africa. Christ has empowered us to establish ministry sites in Uganda, Kenya, Sudan, Rwanda, Nigeria, Tanzania, and Cameroon. We have gone from the smallest towns to the largest cities, and only just begun with the great need for theological training. We create seminaries, pastors, and churches which create disciples. We are dreaming of Kingdom growth, of the unreached being reached, of tens of thousands of churches being planted and the explosion of the Christian Church. We are dreaming of the Kingdom of God covering the earth and are dreaming of Africa where the Christian faith transforms the culture. This week we had the great blessing of receiving a phone call from Pete saying I am in Hawaii. Yesterday we had lunch in our home and Pete inspired us more than he ever did before, he now has 7 locations in Africa, a completed dormitory for 180 students increased the power for the radio stations in Kapchorwa, Uganda, and purchased additional stations in Nigeria and Cameroon, a new clinic ,a library, and an administration building, in Uganda, we have sent a team to plant a Bible Institute in the Congo, we purchased a van for students between campuses we have begun a Bible Institute in Tanzania, our students are busy planting new churches. We need help with the cost of training pastors. We work in an area of Tanzania (one of the worlds poorest nations), there are 50 million people comprised of more than 150 indigenous ethnic groups, Church leadership development is our top priority there. Witchcraft is widespread in all Africa. Pete is one of the humblest men I ever met.

Louis Marie Cordonnier (516)

Louis Marie Cordonnier was born July 7, 1854 in Haubourdin in the French Flanders Region. He studied architecture at the Ecole des Beaux-Arts in Paris and returned to Lille for his first major commission, the 1881 town hall of Loos, (located in Nord in the regions of Hauts at the northern French border); his chosen style was a strongly regional Flemish Renaissance Revival in red brick, with a characteristic belfry tower. In his career he designed Opera de Lille, Basillica of St Therese Lisieux, and many more. His best-known work was the design of the Peace Palace in The Hague, (now the International Court of Justice), which is the principal judicial body of the United Nation. For centuries continents have been torn apart by wars, raw images of battlefields have long been a motivation to look for better solutions than the use of the sword especially as weapons became more deadly. At the peace conference in The Hague in 1899, it was at the initiative of the Russian Czar Nicholas II, that a peace palace should be erected; 26 countries gathered at that conference, to discuss disarmament, international jurisdiction, and arbitration. In order to find a suitable design, the conference organized a foundation, to begin an open international competition in search of a suitable architecture. The winning design that was chosen became an immediate challenge; it was set in the Neo-Renaissance, and was submitted by French architect Louis Marie Cordonnier, and to build it within budget, *he was assisted by* his Dutch associate, J.A.G. van der Steur who adjusted the design. As a sign of their support, the palace was filled with gifts of the nations who had attended the second peace conference. Some of the gifts, (such as Persian rugs, Danish doors, Italian marble), came from Italy, Persia, Russia, Belgium, Denmark, Switzerland, Japan, Indonesia, and the US. Even though, the building design was chosen by an independent jury, it was so controversial it fueled lawsuits for seven years. In 1907, the second Peace Conference was organized in which 44 countries participated; that time the foundation stone was laid in the presence of the Dutch Royal Family, the building was not only intended to house the Permanent Court of Arbitration, but also to house the largest library in the field of international law and peace. The Carnegie Stichting was founded to fund, build, and manage the building. Construction was completed on 28 August 1913. Of all the buildings designed by Louis Marie Cordonnier, (and he did many), The Peace Palace was the crown on his life's work. He died November 20, 1940 in Peyrillac-et-Millac, France. (*The Peace Palace was an important building to me; it was the subject of my first black and white winning photo in a 1950's photo competition.*

Jay Adams (517)

Jay Edward Adams was born January 30, 1929 in Baltimore Maryland US. His father was a policeman and his mother a secretary. At age 15 he graduated from high school. His father was given a Gideon Testament when he served in the military, Jay found it, read it, and God opened his heart, he studied the Bible and became a pastor in the Bible Presbyterian Church. In 1958 he moved to Missouri to become director of Home Mission, and wrote a book titled _Realized Millennialism_, it generated so much controversy, he decided to resign and focus on his PhD studies at the University of Missouri. In 1963 he moved to New Jersey became the pastor of an Orthodox Presbyterian Church and was invited to teach homiletics at Westminster Theological Seminary. He was assigned a course titled "_Poimenics_". (Pastoral theology), and was expected to teach pastoral counseling. There was no material about Christian counseling, all other seminaries used secular and pagan concepts, but Jay would not do that, and began designing Biblical material. This resulted in being introduced as a man who has never had an unpublished thought; it was more real than witty. Some time ago he was our house guest for a week while we were in the middle of a major remodeling project; the workers had just installed all the interior walls with new drywall. We were still of two minds, should we paint, or do wallpaper? While Adams stayed at our home, he confessed that his real dream was never to be a pastor or counselor, but always wanted to be a cartoonist and asked would you mind if I draw some cartoons on your dry walls while you are waiting on paint or wallpaper; he said the temptation is great and these walls are begging for a cartoonist, it will be a tremendous release to practice my boyhood dreams, and you may be the only homeowner that allows me to write on your walls. We said okay, and it became obvious that Jay was in his element filling all the walls with very artistic and professional cartoons so beautiful that we almost considered keeping it as is. But then the inevitable reality hit us like ton of bricks; we decided on some wall paper and some paint. When the wallpaper-glue and the paint had dried, all the cartoons bled through and we were compelled to bring in professionals and do the entire project again and discovered that life is a matter of _live and learn_. It is still an honor to have known Dr. Jay Adams as a personal friend. On November 14, 2020 Jay Adams died, leaving behind more than 100 books some being scholarly seminary study books; his best-known book is a large volume titled: "_Competent to Counsel_" which is a classic. Jay Adams is often referred to as the Dean of Christian Counseling, using only scriptural principles; he has written books on hermeneutics, Christian living, devotional, and books on preaching. Jay Adams is considered the pioneer of Christian counseling.

John Bunyan (518)

John Bunyan's birth date is not known but he was baptized on 30 November 1628 in the village of Elstow, Bedfordshire England; the baptismal entry in the parish registers reading: *John the sonne of Thomas Bunyan*. The reason for the undefinitive birth date is because the record office of Bedfordshire indicates 34 variants of the name Bunyan. It most likely had its origin in the Norman French name Bunnion. His father was a brazier or tinker who traveled in the area mending pots and pans. John picked up swearing from his father. In the summer of 1644, he lost both his mother and his sister Margaret. John had some schooling and at the age of 16 joined the Parliamentary Army during the first stage of the Civil War. After that he returned as a tinker, (*mostly an unskilled person*). He was married about that time, but the name of his wife is not known. He became interested in religion joined a non-conformist group in Bedford, and became a preacher. After the restoration of the monarch the freedom of nonconformists was curtailed and Bunyan was arrested and spent the next 12 years in jail for refusing to give up preaching. In jail he began writing his most famous work "*The Pilgrim's Progress*" which was not published until several years after his release. The book also became an influential literary model, and was translated in more than 200 languages; it had gained immediate popularity, by 1692, (four years after the author's death), 100,000 copies had been printed in England, France, and Holland, and by 1938, 250 years after Bunyan's death more than 1,300 editions of the book had been printed and was estimated to have sold around 250 million copies. In addition to *Pilgrim's Progress*, Bunyan wrote sixty titles, many of them were his expanded sermons. After he had served his prison time, in most of his years later, he lived in relative comfort as a popular English author, pastor, and Puritan preacher, of the Bedford Meeting. Bunyan's work, in particular *The Pilgrim's Progress,* has reached a wider audience through stage and productions, film, TV, and radio. John Bunyan had six children, five of whom are known to have married, of whom four had children. The museum of Elstow has a record of John's descendents, down to the nineteenth century, but as of 2013, no verifiable trace of later descendents has been found. Among his many works are: A few signs from Hell, (1658) ; Christ a Complete Savior, (1692); Come and Welcome to Jesus Christ, (1678); Grace Abounding to the Chief of Sinners, (1666); Praying with the Spirit and with Understanding too, (1663); Of Antichrist and his ruin, (1692); Saved by Grace, (1675); and many more. John Bunyan died at age 59 on 31 August 1688. He is remembered in the Church of England and is on the liturgical calendar of the US Episcopal Church on 29 August.

C. S. Lewis (519)

Clive Staples Lewis (commonly known as C. S. Lewis), was born 29 Nov. 1898 in Belfast in Ulster, Ireland. His dog Jacksie was killed by a car when he was 4 years old, after that he insisted to be called Jacksie, later changed it to Jack. He was a Tutor, Lay theologian, Fellow, and British writer; held academic positions in English Literature at Oxford Univ. Magdalen College and Cambridge University, and is best known for his works of fiction. Lewis was one of the intellectual giants of the twentieth century and arguably one of the most influential writers of his day. In 1954 he was unanimously elected to be chair of Medieval and Renaissance Literature at Cambridge University, a position he held until his retirement, only a few months before he died. Lewis wrote more than thirty books, most distinguished and very popular, were <u>*The Screw tape Letters, the Chronicles of Narnia*</u> and <u>*The Space Trilogy*</u>, and for his non-fiction Christian apologetics, such as <u>Mere Christianity, Miracles,</u> and <u>The Problem of Pain.</u> Just the <u>*Chronicles of Narnia*</u> alone have sold over 100 million copies and have been transformed in to three major motion pictures. Lewis had drifted away from religion but returned to Anglicanism at age 32 due to his friend Tolkien and some other friends, he became an "<u>ordinary layman of the Church of England</u>". Lewis's faith profoundly affected his work, and his wartime radio broadcasts on the subject of Christianity brought him wide acclaim; his books have been translated into more than 30 languages and have sold millions of copies. The Chronicles of Narnia have sold the most and have been popularized on stage, TV, radio, and cinema. In there it was clear that *<u>Aslan</u>* represents Christ and his sacrifice on the table clearly is about the crucifixion. His philosophical writings are widely cited by Christian apologetics from a great variety of many denominations. Lewis read and appreciated a lot of literature; he himself read much of the lively children's stories of Edith Nesbit who wrote a lot of Ghost stories, he loved reading these stories and urges young people to do much reading and use imagination. In 1956, at his age 58, he married American writer Joy Davidman; the marriage was short lived, Joy died of cancer 4 years later at age 45. These are some of C. S. Lewis's quotes: "You are never too old to dream another dream" "Education without value makes man a cleverer devil." "If you love deeply, you are going to get hurt badly, but it's still worth it." "True humility is not thinking less of yourself, it is thinking of yourself less." "There is no neutral ground in the Universe; every inch is already claimed by God". "Some day you will be old enough to start reading Fairy Tales again." C. S. Lewis died on 22 November 1963 from kidney failure, just one week before his 65th birthday.

John Owen (520)

John Owen was born in 1616 in Stadhampton in Oxfordshire England. He was a nonconformist and was educated at Queens College, Oxford, at the time the college was noted, (*according to Thomas Fuller*), for its metaphysicians. Owens was a Puritan by upbringing; in 1637 he was driven out of Oxford by Bishop Laud's new statutes, (Laud was the archbishop of Canterbury and was intolerant of anyone who had opposing views, so much so it escalated in the bishop's riots in Scotland, he was willing to persecute anyone who opposed him. His persecution zeal backfired and Bishop William Laud was impeached and beheaded on 10 January, 1645, I wish no harm on a Bishop who lived 600 yrs ago, but question, is this perhaps something English literary critic Thomas Rymer had in mind when he coined the phrase "*poetic justice*"?). John Owen became chaplain and tutor in the family of Sir Robert Dormer and later in that of Lord Lovelace. At the outbreak of the English Civil War, he sided with the parliament, and thus lost his place and the prospect of succeeding to the Welsh Royalist uncle's fortune. For a while he lived in Charterhouse Yard, troubled by religious questions. His doubts were removed hearing a sermon preached by a stranger in the church of St Mary Aldermanbury where he had gone intending to hear Edmund Calamy the Elder, Owen's first publication, the display of Arminianism (senergism) (1642) was a spirited defence of Calvinism (monergism). It was dedicated to the committee of religion and gained him the living of Fordham in Essex, from which a scandalous minister had been ejected. He remained there engrossed in the work of his parish and writing only *the duty of Pastors* and *People Distinguished* until 1646. In 1644, Owen married Mary Rooke; the couple had 11 children, 10 of whom died in infancy. Owens became pastor at Coggeshall in Essex with a large influx of Flemish tradesman. His adoption of Congregational principles did not affect his theological position he often had long arguments and debates with Richard Baxter, another Puritan pastor. Owen was chosen to preach to parliament on the day after the execution of King Charles I who was beheaded on Saturday Jan. 30, 1649 outside the Banqueting House in Whitehall; he was found guilty by the high court of justice to uphold in himself unlimited tyrannical power to rule according to his will and overthrow the rights and liberties of the people. Owen preached for sincerity of religion in high places. The reaction of other European nations was mostly negative, only Russia broke off diplomatic relations with England. Owen showed himself a firm disciplinarian and won many thanks of parliament, but also the friendship of Oliver Cromwell who took him to Ireland as his chaplain. John Owen died at age 66 August 1683 in England.

Richard Baxter (521)

Richard Baxter was born 12 November 1615 in Row ton, Shropshire, England. His early education was poor being mainly in the hands of the local clergy, themselves virtually illiterate. He got help from John Owen and made some progress in Latin. On Owen's advice he did not go to Oxford, which he regretted later. Instead, he was reluctantly persuaded to go to court in London, he went but soon returned home resolved to study divinity, especially more so by the death of his mother. Baxter read theology with Francis Garbet, the local clergyman, and was ordained and licensed by the Bishop of Worcester... In 1638, Baxter became master of the free grammar school at Dudley, where he commenced his ministry as a Puritan preacher. His success was at first small but soon he established a great reputation relating to nonconformity in the Church of England and it did not take long for him to be alienated from the Church on these issues. He established a reputation for vigorously discharging the duties of his office, and remained at Bridgnorth for nearly 2 years, during which time he took a special interest in the controversy relating to Nonconformity, and the Church of England which was much deeper than just one issue, there were several matters, he rejected, such as episcopacy in its English form, especially the _Etcaetera Oath_, which was the oath taken by every clergyman: "_..I approve the doctrine and discipline of the Church of England_..." it was obvious, being a nonconformist, <u>he did not</u>. Non conformists were protestant Christians who did not conform to the governance and usages of the established church, subsequently his ministry bas beset with interruptions for 19 years. He was exposed to annoyances as well as great danger. He was forced to temporarily retire and was preaching to the soldiers. His connection to the Parliamentary Army was characteristic of his situation. He regretted that he had not previously accepted Cromwell's offer to become chaplain. In 1650 he was ill but kept busy writing. After recovering he became more of a prominent political leader which got him in more controversy. As he approached seventy, he spent 18 moths in prison. When his health deteriorated, he wrote about 168 works including the _Methodus Theologiae Christianae_. (In there he set forth most of his theology). He rejected limited atonement which drew him in to a long debate with Calvinist John Owen. According to records Richard Baxter wrote at least 141 books. The German Sociologist Max Weber made significant use of Baxter's works in developing his thesis for Protestant Ethics. Baxter's home on High Street is still there bearing a plaque which reads: "_In a stormy divided age he advocated unity and comprehension pointing the way to the everlasting rest_." Richard Baxter, after a life filled with turbulence died at age 76 on 8 December 1691 in London.

Hugo Junkers (522)

Hugo Junkers was born February 3, 1859 in Rheydt, Rhine Province Kingdom of Prussia, (now Germany). He attended the Royal Polytechnic University in Charlottenburg and the Royal Technical University in Aachen, where he completed his engineering studies in 1883. He then attended further lectures on electromagnetism and thermodynamics held by Adolf Slaby in Charlottenburg, Slaby placed him with the Comtinental-Gasgesellschaft in Dessau where he worked on the development on the first opposed-piston engine. To measure heating value, he patented a calorimeter and entered it in the 1893 World's Columbian Exposition in Chicago, where it was awarded a gold medal. The next year he patented a gas-fired bath boiler, which refined as a tankless heater. In order to utilize his inventions, in 1895 he founded Junkers and Co. In 1897 he was offered a professorship of mechanical engineering at Aachen, where he lectured until 1912. Although he was lecturing in class he kept working as an engineer at the same time, and devised, patented, and exploited, calorimeters, domestic appliances (gas stoves), pressure regulators, gas oil engines, fan heaters, and other inventions. He began working with engineer Hans Reissner in Aachen; Reissner had developed an all-metal aircraft on which work had first started in 1909 at the Brand Heath, equipped with corrugated iron wings built by Junkers and Co in Dessau. The iron wings were patented one year later. Junkers had a wind tunnel built and invented a hydraulic brake. Hugo had far-sighted ideas of metal aero planes and flying wings, but the necessities of the war (1914-1918) held him back, which was (World War I), he was an engineer and not a warrior but was committed to the fatherland and when the government forced him to focus on aircraft production, he was reluctant about it, but complied. In 1915, he developed the World's first practical all metal aircraft design, the Junkers J 1 "Blechesel" (*Sheet metal donkey*). Which survived on display in Deutsches Museum in Munich until WWII? His firm's first military production design in 1916-17 was the armored-fuselage, two-seat, all metal sesquiplane known by its *idFlieg* designation, the Junkers J.I, considered the best German ground attack aircraft of the war. During this time the German government forced him to merge with Anthony Fokker to form the Junkers-Fokker Aktiengesesellschaft on 20 October 1917. Postwar Soviet aviation pioneer Andrei Tupolev, and American aviation designer William Bushnell Stout owed much to Hugo Junkers's construction technique. Hugo was a true engineering polymath who designed many successful aircraft. In 1976 he was inducted into the International Air and Space Hall of Fame. On his 76th birthday, Hugo Junkers died February 3, 1935 in Gauting, Bavaria, Germany.

Christiane Amanpour (523)

Christiane Maria Amanpour was born 12 January 1958 in England at a West London Suburb, and was raised in Tehran until age 11. Her father was Iranian a Shi'ite Muslim and her mother was Catholic. After her primary school in England, she attended Holy Cross Convent, an all-girls school in England, at age 16, New Hall School, a Catholic school in Essex. The family lived in Iran when the (Islamic Revolution, (Iran-Iraq War) began, they returned to England and remained there; but Christiane moved to the U.S. to study journalism at the University of Rhode Island. There, she worked in the news department at WBRU-FM in Providence, and also worked for NBC as an electronic graphics designer. In 1983 she graduated from the university *summa cum laude* and Phi Beta Kappa with a B.A. degree in journalism, and was hired by CNN on the foreign desk in Atlanta Georgia, as an entry-level desk assistant. Her first major assignment was covering Iran-Iraq War, which led to her being transferred in 1986 to Eastern Europe to report on the fall of European communism. In 1989, she was assigned to work in Frankfurt am Main in Germany, where she reported on the democratic revolutions sweeping Eastern Europe. Through this position, she was able to move up in the company and by 1990 served as a correspondent for CNN's New York bureau. Following Iraq's occupation of Kuwait in 1990, Amanpour's reports of the Persian Gulf War brought her wide notice while also taking CNN to a new level of news coverage. Then she reported on the Bosnian war and other conflict zones. Because of her emotional delivery during the Siege of Sarajevo, viewers and critics questioned her professional objectivity, claiming that many of her reports favored the Bosnian Muslims, to which she replied, "<u>*There are some situations one simply cannot be neutral about, because when you are neutral you are an accomplice. Objectivity means giving each side a hearing.*</u>" From1992 to 2010 she was CNN's chief international correspondent as well as the anchor of *Amanpour*, <u>a daily CNN interview program that aired 2009-2010.</u> She has reported on the world's major crisis and hotspots, including Iraq, Afghanistan, Palestine, Iran, Israel, Pakistan, Somalia, Rwanda, the Balkans, and the United States during hurricane Katrina. She has interviewed presidents and leaders such as Tony Blair, Jacques Chirac, Nicolas Maduro, Angela Merkel, Dalai Lama, Moammar Gadhaffi and many others. She has had many memorable moments in her career; and questioned intervention in Syria. She is a member of the Council of Foreign Relations and the Institute for War and Peace Reporting, and served as a UNESCO Goodwill Ambassador. She holds more than 20 recognitions and honorary degrees. Amanpour gained a reputation of being fearless for reporting from conflict areas.

Mary Todd Lincoln (524)

Mary Ann Todd Lincoln was born December 13, 1818 in Kentucky U.S, to Robert Smith Todd, a banker, and Elizabeth Todd. Her parents were slave-owners and Mary was raised in comfort; she was 6 when her mother died in childbirth. Two years later her father married Elizabeth Humphreys they had 9 children together. Mary had a difficult relationship with her stepmother. At an early age she was schooled with a curriculum of French (which she spoke fluently), and literature. She studied dance, drama, music. By age 20 she was witty and gregarious. She was a Whig. Mary lived with her sister Elizabeth in Springfield, who was married to Ninian W. Edwards, son of a former governor, he was Mary's guardian. She was popular with the gentry of Springfield, and was courted by a young lawyer and Democratic Party politician Stephen A. Douglas; she chose Abraham Lincoln, a fellow Whig and married him on November 4, 1842, at her sister Elizabeth's home. She was 23 years old and he was 33. They had four sons Robert, Edward, William, and Thomas. While Lincoln was increasingly more successful as a young lawyer, Mary supervised the household. The home where they resided from 1844 until 1861, still stands in Springfield and has been designated a National Historic Site. Lincoln was a circuit lawyer, and Mary was often left alone for months to run the household. She supported her husband socially and politically even more so after he was elected president. She cooked simple meals for him often. The nation was deeply divided over slavery and many other difficulties. While in the White House she often visited hospitals with flowers and fruit. The papers announced that the president would attend the theatre, but Mary suffered from severe headaches often, although she felt she should go with her husband and in the theater while they were holding hands, John Wilkes Booth fired a shot that struck the back of his head. Their oldest son Robert was with them and stayed with his mom and dad through the night although Lincoln died about 7 AM, the next morning he was 56. Mary received condolence messages from all over the world most of whom she answered personally; including a very moving letter from Queen Victoria who had lost her husband Albert only 4 years earlier. The death of Lincoln and one of her boys brought on overpowering grief, Mary suffered much of her life from severe headaches depression. After Lincoln's death she lived with one of her son's but had serious depressions for the remainder of her life. Mary died at age 63 on July 16, 1882 in Springfield Illinois.

Sarah Palin (525)

Sarah Louise Palin was born 11 February 1964 in Sandpoint Idaho, the third of four children, being English, Irish and German ancestry. The family relocated to Eagle River, Alaska, and settled in Skagway when she was a few months old, meaning she grew up in Alaska, and attended Junior High and High School and Wasilla High School where she was head of Fellowship of Christian Athletes and a member of the girls basketball and cross-country running teams. During her senior year, she was co-captain and point guard of the basketball team that won the 1982 Alaska state championship, earning the nickname "*Sarah Barracuda*" for her competitive streak. In 1984, Palin won the Miss Wasilla beauty pageant and finished 3rd as second runner up in Miss Alaska pageant where she won the title of "Miss Congeniality". She played the flute in the talent portion of the contest. After graduating from high school in 1982, she enrolled in the University of Hawaii in Hilo, and later transferred to Hawaii Pacific University in Honolulu for a semester in the fall of 1982. After that enrolled in North Idaho Community College, in 1985 she went back to Alaska and worked as a sportscaster for KTUU-TV and KTVA-TV in Anchorage; and as a sports reporter for the Mat-Su-Valley Frontiersman, fulfilling an early ambition. In August 1988, she eloped with Todd Palin, her high school sweetheart, and after their first baby she helped him in the commercial fishing business. Then she got ambitious, tried politics and was elected to the Wasilla City Council in 1992, winning 530/310 votes. All this time she remained loyal to the Republican Party, and set her sites a little higher in state offices. Governor Murkowski offered her positions in the Alaska Oil and Gas but she had no background in that area. Then she ran against Frank Murkowski in the Republican Gubernatorial election and won becoming the first female governor of Alaska at age 42. At first, she was successful but after a while her popularity declined, although she was supportive of drilling for oil and natural gas. She frequently broke with the Alaska Republican establishment, and publicly challenged US Senator Ted Stevens to come clean in his financial dealings and soon after Stevens was indicted. She made an attempt to run as a vice president on the John Mc Cain ticket but it was not a success. She may have served above her pay grade but was willing to offer herself and make a difference. Sarah Palin's personal life was not without challenges. Todd filed for divorce in August 2019 citing incompatibility of temperament; the divorce was finalized on March 23, 2020 Why is she here? She was a concerned housewife in Alaska and decided to get involved and succeeded to capture a seat in the highest office in the State of Alaska serving there as governor from 2006 to 2009; not a small accomplishment.

Maria Sharapova (526)

Maria Sharapova was born 19 April 1987 Nyagan Russia. Although she is Russian, she has lived in the United States since age seven. When she was three the family moved to Sochi Krasdodar Krai and at age four she hit her first tennis ball. Her father Yuri befriended Alexandr Kafelnikov, whose son Yevgenie would go on to win two grand slam singles title and became Russias first No 1 ranked tennis player. Alexandr gave Sharapova her first tennis racket in 1991 when she was four and began practicing with her father at a local park. Maria took her first professional lessons with veteran coach Yuri Yutkin, who was instantly impressed when he saw her play, noting her exceptional hand-eye coordination. In 1993, at age six, Sharapova attended a tennis clinic in Moscow run by Martina Navratilova who recommended professional training with Nick Bolletieri at the IMG Academy in Florida. With borrowed money he and his daughter went to Florida, neither could speak English. In 1994 she began training with Rick Macci. In 1995 she signed by IMG who saw a star and agreed to pay the annual tuition fee of $35,000 for her to stay at the Academy at age nine; she went on to debuts, with her best performance of two Junior Grand Slam events in Australia, and Wimbledon. Throughout her career her greatest asset was her mental toughness and competitive spirit. She now has a home in Bradenton Florida and in Manhattan Beach California. From 2005 to 2011 Sharapova was named to the Forbes Celebrity 100, which compiles the top 100 most powerful celebrities of that year. She became the world no 1 tennis player on 22 August 2005 at age 18 becoming the first Russian female player to hold that title. She last held that ranking for the 5th time for 4 weeks from 11 June 2012 to 8 July 2012. She won five grand slam titles, two at the French open, and one each at the Australian open, Wimbledon, and the US Open, winning 36 titles in total, including the year-ending WTA Finals in her debut in 2004. She has appeared in advertisements, including Nike, Prince, and Canon, and has been featured in a number of modeling assignments, including Sports Illustrated. Since February 2007, she has been a United Nations Ambassador for the Development Programme Goodwill, concerned specifically for the Chernobyl Recovery and Development Programme. In June 2011 she was named one of the 30 Legends of Women's Tennis: Past, Present and Future by *Time* and in March 2012 were named one of the "100 Greatest of All Time" by *Tennis Channel*. According to Forbes, she has been named highest-paid female athlete of the world for 11 consecutive years and earned $285 million prize money since she turned pro in 2001. She is fully ready to pay back and in 2018 she launched a new program to mentor women entrepreneurs. Her autobiography is appropriately titled <u>Unstoppable.</u>

Louisa May Alcott (527)

Louisa May Alcott was born 29 Nov. 1832 in Germantown, now a suburb of Philadelphia U.S. She was the second of four girls, and was a tomboy, preferring boy games. In 1834 the family moved to Boston where they established an experimental school but Louise joined a boy's club. The school was not a success and the family moved to a cottage situated along the Sudbury River in Concord Massachusetts. In her early education, which she described later as mostly from her father who was strict and believed in self-denial; she also received some instruction from people like Ralph Waldo Emerson, Margaret Fuller, and Julia Ward Howe, all of whom were family friends. The 1850's were tough years, there was much tension on both sides of the slavery issue, and families were torn apart. Her family served as station masters in <u>The Underground Railroad</u>, *(A network of secret routes and safe houses established in the US during the early- to mid-19th century, used by enslaved African Americans, primary to escape into free states and Canada, assisted by abolitionists and others sympathetic to the cause of the escapees; there were also routes to Mexico and the Caribbean. It was open until the Emancipation Proclamation was signed by President Lincoln on 1 January 1863 changing the Federal legal status of 3.5 million enslaved Americans. It is estimated that 100,000 have escaped using the network.)* Alcott had to go to work at an early age as a seamstress, domestic helper, teacher, governess and writer; many families experienced much stress during the civil war and for her, writing became a creative and emotional outlet. Her first book: <u>Flower Fables (1849)</u>, a selection of tales written for Ellen Emerson. In 1847 while serving on the Underground Railroad they housed fugitive slaves for a week and worked closely with Frederick Douglass. Women did not experience as much freedom as they enjoyed 100 years later. In 1858 her younger sister Elizabeth died, it felt like a breaking up their sisterhood and along with all the pressures of the Civil War she was so filled with despair, Alcott contemplated suicide. As an adult she was an abolitionist and a feminist. *<u>(A woman 100 years ago, had virtually no rights, a feminist had a totally different meaning than it has today</u>)*. She wrote in her journal that she frequently enjoyed going on long walks and runs. Her home, where the family lived for 25 years, and where she wrote <u>Little Women</u> (1868) has been a historic house museum since 1912 and they are remembered for their contribution to public education; her Boston home is featured on the Boston Women's Heritage Trail. She wrote for the Atlantic Monthly when the Civil War broke out, and served as a nurse in the Union Hospital in Georgetown DC. Louise Alcott died of a stroke at age 55 on March 6, 1888 in Boston 2 days after her father's death.

Margaret (Peggy) Garner (528)

Margaret Garner was born into a house of slavery as an African American woman, and was a mulatto woman meaning she was partially white, a clear indication that the real father was the slave owner. Peggy later killed her own daughter, rather than allow the child returned to slavery. The family had escaped in January 1856 it was the coldest winter in 60 years; and traveled across the frozen Ohio River to Cincinnati, but were apprehended by US Marshals acting under the Fugitive Slave Act of 1850. Her defense attorney John Jolliffe moved to have her tried for murder in Ohio, a move to get her to a free state. Garner's story is so moving it became the inspiration of the novel <u>Beloved</u> (1987) by Nobel Prize-winning author Toni Morrison. She may have been the daughter of Plantation Owner John Pollard Gaines of Boone County Kentucky. In 1849 she married Robert Garner an enslaved man. That December, along with all the people enslaved there were sold to John P. Gaines's younger brother Archibald K. Gaines. The first child of Peggy was born in 1850, but the younger 3 children were mulattoes. Peggy had visible scars on her head of having been beaten and the younger 3 children were Archibald's children. When in January 1856 they escaped Margaret was pregnant, there were 17 in their party making a dash for freedom. Her husband Robert had stolen his enslaver's horses and sleigh and his gun, at daybreak all 17 crossed the frozen river, and to avoid detection they divided. The Garners and their 4 children with Roberts's father made it to the home of Margaret's uncle Joe Kite, a former slave himself. The other nine people reached safe houses and eventually escaped via Underground Railroad to Canada. Kite went to abolitionist Levi Coffin for advice on how to get the group to safety. Coffin agreed to help them escape the city and told Kite to take the Garner group further west of the city, where many free black people lived. Slave catchers and US Marshals found the Garners, they surrounded the property and stormed the house. Robert fired shots and wounded a Marshal; Margaret killed her two-year-old daughter with a butcher knife rather then let her return to slavery. She wounded her other children and intended to kill herself but was captured and subdued by the posse. The defense attorney pointed out that Margaret's action was driven by the severe abuse she had endured at the hands of the slave owners. The courtroom was packed every day. The pale faces of the children told the real story. Margaret lost in court and was forced back to slavery and escaped again on a steamboat but the boat collided with another boat and sunk in the river Margaret drowned her baby then attempted to do the same for her family. After that they disappeared from site, she is beleved to have died from typhoid fever, and urged Robert to never marry again in slavery.

Jessica (Jessi) Combs (529)

Jessi Combs was born July 27, 1980 in Rockerville South Dakota U.S. the daughter of Jamie Combs and Nina Darrington. The family moved to Piedmont, South Dakota when she was two years old. She had 2 siblings, Kelly Combs and Danielle Theis, and three step-siblings, Rebekah Hall and Austin Darrington Combs' great-grandmother was Nina DeBow, a jazz pianist who raced Stanley Steamers. Jessi graduated from Stevens High School in 1998. After high school Jessi got a full scholarship to an interior design school and moved to Denver to pursue a career in snowboarding. Shortly thereafter she found the sport to be too physically demanding for her taste, and decided to move to Laramie, Wyoming to study Collision Refinishing. Chassis Fabrication Street Rod Fabrication and Upholstery at the WyoTech College, she started to develop a passion for vehicles. After that she graduated from WyoTech in 2004, where she attended the Collision and Refinishing Core Program, the Street Rod Fabrication and Custom Fabrication and High-Performance Powertrain programs. Following her graduation, Combs first professional job came after the WyoTech marketing; department hired her and another student, to build a car from the ground up in six months to debut at the Specialty Equipment Marketing Association's (SEMA) show. At the same time, she hosted the Spike Television show Xtreme 4x4, a part of the powerblock for four years. Following an on-set accident she announced in February 2008 that she would leave the show. In 2009, Combs appeared in twelve episodes of the seventh season of Myth busters while Kari Byron was on maternity leave. She also appeared on overhaulin. In 2011 she hosted Autoblog: *100 car things to do before you die.* From 2011 to 2014 she hosted *all girls garage*. It was a show of repairing and upgrading classic cars. In 2018 she was featured on Discovery Channel on a show called Break Room. She built her own race cars and had a passion to break her own land speed record which was 512.71 mph. She finally did at Alvord Desert in southeastern Oregon as part of the American Eagle Project on a dry lake bed while driving her converted airplane, (wings removed.) On August 27 2019 she reached 522.783 mph (841.338km/h. *It was her last ride* as she was nearing 550 mph when a failure of a front wheel, (likely caused by hitting an object in the desert), which caused the front wheel assembly to collapse at that speed. The car crashed and burned in a blazing fire, with Jessi strapped inside, it engulfed the race vehicle after the crash. The speed record was verified by Guinness World Record in June 2020. Jessi died the way she lived and reached her dream, although she did not enjoy it.

Elizabeth Freeman (530)

Elizabeth Freeman (also known as Mum Beth), was born in slavery around 1744. at the farm of Pieter Hogeboom in New York, where she was given the name Bet. When their daughter Hannah married John Ashley, they gave Bet (around seven years old) to Hannah and her husband. She remained with them until 1781, during which time she had a child, she had no husband. Throughout her life, Bet exhibited a strong spirit and sense of self. She had many conflicts with Hanna who was raised in strict culture. In 1780, Bet prevented Hannah from striking a servant girl with a heated shovel; Elizabeth shielded the girl and received a deep wound in her arm. As the wound healed, she left it uncovered as evidence of her harsh treatment, and had a bad arm all winter. When people said to her – Why Betty! she answered - ask mistress. John Ashley was a Yale educated lawyer, wealthy landowner, businessman, and leader in the community. His house was the site of many political discussions and the probable location of the signing of the Sheffield Resolves, which predated the Declaration of Independence. In 1780, Freeman either heard the newly ratified constitution read at a public gathering in Sheffield, or overheard her master talking in the home. This is what she heard; <u>All men are born free and equal, and have certain natural , essential and unalienable rights; among which may be reckoned the right of enjoying and defending their lives and liberties; that of acquiring, possessing, and protecting property; in fine, that of seeking and obtaining their safety and happiness.</u> (*Article 1, of Massachusetts Constitution*.) Inspired by these words she sought the counsel of Theodore Sedgwick, a young abolition-minded lawyer, to help her sue for freedom in court. After much deliberation he accepted the case, and that of Brom, another of Ashley's slaves. He enlisted the aid of the Founder of <u>Litchfield Law School</u>, one of America's earliest law schools, located in Litchfield Connecticut. The case went to trial and the jury decided that Bet should be paid thirty shillings and return to the Ashley family. She refused, and grew fond of Sedgwick family, (the lawyer who helped her), and worked for him. Bet changed her name to Elizabeth Freeman and worked for the Sedgwick family, many years, and became incredibly close to them, even saved enough money to buy her own house where she lived and raised her family. She was born a slave, and remained a slave for thirty years. She could neither read nor write. She never violated a trust, nor failed to perform her duty. In every situation she was the most efficient helper and most tender friend, and was a good mother. After she gained her freedom, she became widely recognized and in demand for her skills as a healer, midwife and nurse. She lived to her mid eighties and died on 28 December, 1829 and was buried in the Sedgwick family plot.

Lady Jane Grey (9-day Queen) (531)

Jane Dudley was a teenage English noblewoman in succession to the British throne of England and Ireland. She was the granddaughter of Henry VII through his younger daughter Mary. (If you have been reading my books 1, 2, and now 3, you may be confused, why her story is here, and may think I am opposed to Death Penalty; then you are wrong, although I am strongly opposed to the reasons in England as cited here. Hawaii re-considered the issue on March 14, 1977, in a televised debate before the full State Legislature, I was chosen by ranking Senator Kawasaki to present the case in favor, and an ACLU attorney argued against it; neither of us changed a single vote.) The Bible requires it for murder, long before the Mosaic Law, (Gen.9:6). Chuck Colson said: ("*Its justice, if equally applied*). Back to Lady Jane Grey, did she commit murder? No! She was a little girl that inherited the British Throne at age 14, and there were many power-hungry leaders who lost out, in their lust to be a part of the ruling Monarch's power at that time. In my younger days, living in Europe, I was disgusted by such action of Bishops and Cardinals, most of whom were Biblically illiterate. Lady Jane was young, but had an excellent education and a reputation of being one of the most learned young women of her day. She was a committed Protestant and supported the Reformed Church of England, (that alone could have ended her life). To be in succession of the British throne sounds great, but for her it was deadly. When King Edward VI died 10 July 1553, Jane was proclaimed Queen and while awaiting Coronation it was revealed that he had nominated his half sister Mary to be Queen. To be in succession to the British throne is about as confusing as is the Democratic Party in America is today. We all know that Biden is not in charge, but his handlers are; so, it was in England in 1553. These two young ladies were at the mercy of their handlers, which were the Bishops, Lords, and Cardinals. Lady Jane had made a deep commitment to her Savior Jesus, and was the Queen of England for just 9 days. England could not sentence an innocent Queen to death therefore she was convicted of high treason, and sentenced to death. She committed herself to the executioner, walked freely over there and said: "Good people I have come here to die; and wash my hands in innocence before God", and recited Psalm 51. She then blindfolded herself and asked to be taken to the block telling the executioner: *Please do it quickly*, he asked her for forgiveness, which she granted quickly. Her head was then severed in one clean stroke. She was a young 14- or 15-year-old who had more wisdom than those who condemned her. She is featured prominently in Foxes book of Martyrs. There are as many opinions about her life story as there are people in England, but here you have mine.

Cai Lun (532)

Cai Lun (also known as Ts'ai Lun, and Jingzhong, was born about in the year 62; exact date is not known. History indicates that he made a major difference. In China he was a court official who is traditionally credited with the invention of paper. He was a eunuch* (*A castrated human male from remote antiquity, eunuchs were employed in the Middle East and in China in two main functions, as guards of harems or women's quarters, and as chamberlains to kings. They were considered the most suitable guards for the many wives and/or concubines a ruler might have; the confidential position in the harems of princes frequently enabled them to exercise an important influence over their royal masters often had great trust and power. Some rose to become confidential advisers, and even ministers. Some eunuchs underwent castration as a condition of their employment, others it was punishment, some had been sold by poor parents. In China it was common from the Chow period (1122 – 221BC) to the Ming, and Sung dynasties. In Byzantine times of Constantinople, the practice was still there. Then came the Muslim power and after AD 750, and the Ottoman Empire (14 -20th century, there may have been eunuchs in Eastern Europe, Western Asia and Northern Africa. But history was silent about eunuchs after that). Back to Cai Lun, inventor of paper; about the year 105 Cai conceived the idea of forming sheets of paper from the bark of trees. The paper thus obtained was superior in writing quality to cloth, and paper cost less to produce. Cai reported his discovery to the emperor. Before 1798 Nicholas-Louis Robert constructed the first papermaking machine, a few years later the brothers Henry and Seal Fourdrinier improved his machine and in 1809 John Dickinson invented the first cylinder machine. Differences among the grades and types of paper are determined by several factors, such as type of fiber used; the preparation of pulp., either by mechanical (ground wood) or by the addition of other materials to the pulp, among the most common being bleach or coloring and sizing, the latter to retard penetration by ink; by conditions under which the sheet is formed, including its weight, and by the physical or chemical treatments applied to the finished sheet. Weight or substance per unit area called basis weight is measured in reams now commonly 500 sheets. Paper is also measured by caliper (thickness) and density. The strength and durability are determined by many such factors. For money, paper bills were first used by the Chinese, who started carrying folding money during the Tang Dynasty (618-907) and used it more than 500 years before the practice began to catch on in Europe in the 17th century; it took about two centuries for paper money to spread through the rest of the world. In 1455 China ended paper money; and re-adopted it 200 years later.

William R. Dunn (533)

William R. Dunn, commonly referred to as Bill Dunn, was born on 16 November, 1916 in Minneapolis Minnesota. He learned to break wild horses in North Dakota and went on to become a cowboy on the rodeo circuit. At age 12, he had received an airplane and in 1934 a sharp recruiting sergeant convinced Bill, with his flying experience he might be qualified to become an Army Aviation Cadet. Instead of flying he spent 3 years in the infantry and was discharged in 1937, and Bill became a commercial artist, but in 1939 the war broke out and he joined the Canadian military with the assurance he could transfer to the Royal Canadian Air Force, he did and soon transferred to Europe, and was fighting in the battle of Britain in 1940 and soon was flying in Europe; he shot down two German Stuka dive bombers with a Lewis machine gun. His flying experience paid off and earned him a spot as a pilot officer in the Royal Air Force. Following his training, Bill was assigned to RAF 71 Eagle Squadron, made up of American volunteer pilots. On July 2, 1941, flying the Spitfire, Dunn became the first Eagle Squadron pilot to shoot down a German fighter plane; the next month on August 27, 1941 he got four downed German planes to his credit. And was on the tail of a German Me-109 and opened fire. I see the grayish-white tracer streaks from my guns converge on the Messerschmidt's tail section; the elevators and rudders disintegrated under the impact of the explosive DeWild bullets. Pieces were flying of the enemy's fuselage Dunn said the range is now down to 50 yards. Black liquid engine oil spattered his windscreen and a dense brownish colored smoke is flung back at him. His enemy was finished. Splash one but good. He though I've got my fifth victory, but he was attacked by four Me -109's; he was badly wounded and barely made it back to base. The front of his right foot was blown off by a 20 mm cannon shell in addition two machine gun bullets went through his right calf and his skull was grazed by a machine gun bullet. He was sent back to the United States to recover and his time in the Eagle Squadron came to an end. Despite his injuries, Dunn returned to Europe flying P-47 Thunderbolts in the 406-fighter squadron; he shot down more German planes and was wounded again. Having completed two tours in Europe, one with the RAF and one with the US Army Air forces, Dun volunteered for service in the Far East in the China-Burma-India Theater. He flew P-51Mustangs and rose to the rank of Lt Col. Dunn remained in the US Air Force and served a total of 38 years and flew 378 combat missions and will always be remembered as the first American Ace of WW-II. As a hero he set the example how to overcome adversity. He never gave up. Dunn passed away in Colorado in 1995.

E. V. Hill (534)

Edward Victor Hill Sr. was born 10 November, 1933 in Columbus Texas son of William and Rosa Hill. Despite being born in poverty he managed to obtain a four-year scholarship to Prairie View AandM University near Houston to study Agronomy. In 1954 he began pasturing a few Texas churches. While there (together with Martin Luther King) they established the Southern Christian Leadership Conference. He became active in social issues working with government to provide programs, housing, and other amenities for poor of rural blacks. In early 1961 he moved to pastor the Mount Zion Missionary Baptist Church, Los Angeles which became a hotspot of political and social activism in Southern California. Following the 1992 LA riots, President George H.W. Bush visited the church. Hill increasingly aligned himself with the Republican Party in California. He gave the prayer at the Richard Nixon inauguration; and led clergy committees during the presidency of Ronald Reagan. Sometimes he was at odds with other black leaders, but did support Jesse Jackson's 1984 bid for the Democratic Presidential Nomination. He was among the first African-American preachers to broadcast on the Trinity Broadcasting Network and enjoyed considerable influence among the Baptist movement. He served as leader of the State Baptist Convention from 1972, and associate professor of evangelism for the Billy Graham Evangelistic Association, and was also a leading figure in the National Baptist Convention. In 1971 Graham invited him along with seven other black clergymen for a private discussion with then-president Richard Nixon. Other evangelicals with whom he aligned himself were Jimmy Swaggart, and Jerry Falwell. In 1998 he publicly defended the National Baptist Convention's president Henry Lyons, who was ultimately forced to resign. I attended one of Hill's seminars in Los Angeles when he talked about the true gospel. I asked him: "Mr. Hill, you are a popular speaker, who fills your pulpit when you are not here, and what if he is not as true to the Bible as you are?" He gave me an unforgettable answer. This is what he said: "_I can invite anyone to speak in my church, if it not sounds like God; the ladies in my church will stop him._" He was one of the most prominent African-American clergy of his time, Hill was opposed to the term "Black" stating that it was theologically and philosophically unacceptable; he preferred the term "Negro." When his health declined, he was hospitalized at Cedars-Sinai Medical center in Los Angeles with pneumonia and diabetes. At age 69 he died on February 24, 2003 in Los Angeles; the funeral took place at West Los Angeles Cathedral on March 8, 2003 and was attended by 4,000 people, he was a National Civil Rights Leader. His son: E. V. Hill jr. succeeded him as pastor till he died 2019.

Marie Bashkirtseff (535)

Maria Konstantinovna Bashkirtseva was born 12 November 1858 in Gavrontsi Poltava, Russian Empire. To a wealthy noble family, but her parents separated when she was quite young. As a result, she grew up mostly abroad, traveling with her mother throughout most of Europe, spending much time in Germany and on the Riviera until her and her mother finally settled in Paris. Marie died young and lived only to age 25. She was privately educated and with early musical talent, but lost her chance at a career as a singer when illness destroyed her voice. When Marie was compelled to give up singing, she then determined to become an artist, and studied painting at the Robert-Fleury studio, the Academie Julian, in France. That Academie, was one of the few that accepted female students, and it attracted young women from all over Europe and the United States. Fellow students at the Academie included Anna Bilinska-Bohdanowiczowa and Louise Breslau, whom Bashkirtseff viewed as her only real rival; she had been writing her journal from age 12. Her self-portrait was painted about age 13, and has been called a strikingly modern psychological painting and is indicative of a highly gifted mind. She was multilingual and despite her self-involvement, was a keen observer with an acute ear for hypocrisy. A consistent theme throughout the journal is her deep desire to achieve fame, she had a well-founded increasing fear that her intermittent illness might turn out to be tuberculosis. In a prefatory section written toward the end of her life she writes: If I do not die young, I hope to live as a great artist; but if I die young, I intend to have my journal which can not fail to be interesting, published." Similarly; when I am dead, my life, which appears to me a remarkable one, will be read. The only thing wanting is that it should have been different. The first half of Bashkirtseff's journal is a coming-of-age story, while the second half is an account of heroic suffering. Her journal was first published in 1887, (three years after her death). It was an immediate success; not least because of its cosmopolitan confessional style but was a marked departure from the contemplative mystical diaries of the writer Guerin (published in 1862). An English translation appeared two years later under the title <u>Marie Bashkirtseff</u>: *<u>the journal of a young artist 1860-1884.</u>* Translated by Mary Serrano. British Prime Minister William Gladstone referred to her journal as "<u>a book without parallel</u>." Another early admirer was George Bernard Shaw. Her diary was cited as an inspiration by the American writer Mary Mac Lane. Marie worked, and died in Paris; she died at age 25 on 31 October 1884. She herself did not expect to live to an old age. The cause of her death is cited as tuberculosis now reduced or almost eliminated in the developed countries of the world.

Glenn Youngkin (536)

Glenn Allen Youngkin was born 9 December 1966 in Richmond Virginia US. Son of Ellis and Carroll Wayne Youngkin. He was a teenager when the family moved to Norfolk and he graduated from Norfolk Academy in 1985 where he had received numerous basketball honors. He is 6 ft 2 and attended Rice University in Houston, Texas on a basketball scholarship. He played four seasons for the Owls in the Southwest conference and he totaled 82 points and 67 rebounds in his career. In 1990 he graduated with a Bachelor of Arts in managerial studies and a Bachelor of Science in mechanical engineering. He attended Harvard Business School and earned a Masters in Business Administration (MBA) degree in 1994. After graduating from Rice in 1990, Youngkin joined the investment bank First Boston, where he handled mergers and acquisitions and capital market financing. The company was bought out by Credit Swisse and became Credit Swisse First Boston. Youngkin left in 1992 to pursue an MBA. In 1994 after receiving his MBA he joined the management consulting firm McKinsey and Company.

In August 1995 he joined the private-equity firm the Carlyle Group, based in Washington DC initially as a member of the US buyout team; in 1999 he was named partner and managing director and managed the firm's United Kingdom buyout team and global sector, dividing his time between London and Washington. When the chief financial officer left in 2010 Youngkin became interim CFO till 2014.In July 2020 Youngkin announced he would retire and seek the Republican Party of Virginia's nomination for governor; he was endorsed by Senator Ted Cruz. Youngkin won the nomination and stressed his support for president Trump. It was not an easy ride, he had to defeat six other candidates, and after winning his party's nomination Youngkin was endorsed by president Trump. He called that endorsement an honor. In the general election he faced Democratic governor Terry McAuliffe. On November 2, 2021 Youngkin defeated McAuliffe with the vote coming in as: 50.58 – 48.64, a close election, but in such races, there can only be one winner. Youngkin was sworn in as 74th governor of Virginia on 15 January,2022. He took office alongside his Republican ticket mates Lieutenant Governor Winsome Sears, the first woman of color to be elected to statewide office in Virginia and Attorney General Jason Miyares, the first Latino elected to statewide office in the state. On his first day in office, he signed a flurry of executing actions such as: rescinded the mandatory mask wearing in public schools, banned the critical race theory, replace the parole board, create commissions to combat human trafficking, he is solid pro-life.

Martha Gellhorn (537)

Martha Ellis Gellhorn was born 8 November, 1908 in St Louis Missouri US. Her father was a German born gynecologist, and was of Jewish descent. At age 7 she participated in the Golden Lane, (a rally for women's suffrage at the Democratic Party's 1916 National convention in St Louis Missouri.) Women carrying yellow parasols and wearing yellow sashes lined both sides of the main street leading to the St Louis Coliseum, states that had not enfranchised women were standing their draped in black; Gellhorn and another girl Mary Taussich were in front of the line representing future voters. Martha graduated in 1926 from John Burroughs School in St Louis and enrolled in Bryn Mawr College outside Philadelphia, but left without graduating wanting to pursue a career in journalism. Her first published articles appeared in *The New Republic*. In 1930, determined to become a foreign correspondent, she moved to France for two years and worked at the United Press Bureau in Paris, and traveling Europe writing for various newspapers about her experiences and some for her 1934 book: *What Mad Pursuit*. In 1932 she returned to the United States and through friendship met First Lady Eleanor Roosevelt. The Roosevelt's invited her to live at the White House, and hired her as a field investigator for the *Federal Emergency Relief Administration* (FERA), created to help end the Great Depression. In Florida she met Ernest Hemingway, and in 1936 and they traveled to Spain and celebrated Christmas there, married him in 1940. She reported on the rise of Adolf Hitler in Europe; her parents were part German, but she did not like it when soldiers boarded the train and confiscated all her writings. Martha was not happy with the Hitler youth and began reporting on the dangerous fascism she saw on the rise in Europe. It became evident that she had a very low opinion of the Nazis in Europe. When the troops invaded Normandy, she found herself on a hospital ship and had crossed the channel without permission as a part of the Normandy invasion. In Europe she kept hearing about concentration camps and felt compelled to find out more about it. In 1944, lacking press credentials she was able to get in there just before Eisenhower liberated Europe. She got her wish and was able to begin reporting from Dachau. (Her observations were the same as mine after we went in), the brutality and torture that took place there could not be described in human terms, in spite of the fact that the guards were living with their families next door and were able to go home each day; such issues have never been understood. After the war at the trials, all had the same excuse: *Hitler made me do it*. Martha was a passionate and credible war correspondent and kept reporting from the world's trouble spots, even after WW-II. She died in Peace on 15 February, 1998 at age 89 in London.

Jacqueline Cochran (538)

Jacqueline was born Bessie Lee Pittman, in Pensacola, Florida, the youngest of five children. Her family was not wealthy, but there was always food on the table. At age 13-14 she married Robert and gave birth to a son Robert, but he died at age 5. The marriage ended and she became a hairdresser, later moving to New York and got a job at a prestigious salon at Saks Fifth Ave. Her family moved to California and she remarried to a wealthy man. She was offered flying lessons in New York. It turned out Jacqueline was a *natural pilot* and after a few lessons she was flying solo, and within two years got her commercial pilot's license. She became known as Jackie and was one of three women to compete in the Mac Robertson Air Race in 1934. In 1937 she was the only woman to compete in the Bendix race and worked with Amelia Earhart to open that race to women. By 1938 she was considered the best female pilot in America and was the first woman to fly a bomber across the Atlantic. Cochran was often referred to as the speed queen and won five Harmon Trophies. At that time no other woman held more speed, distance, or altitude records in aviation history than Cochran. In September 1939 she wrote to Eleanor Roosevelt, suggesting that a women's flying division be established in the Army Air Forces, with membership of qualified women pilots, who could do most aviation jobs, thereby releasing more male pilots for combat. Cochran was sent to England in 1942 to see how they used female pilots in war time. These efforts resulted in WASP (*Women Air Force Service Pilots*), of which Jackie became the director training hundreds of women pilots in Texas from August 1943 to December 1944. At war's end she witnessed Japanese General Tomoyuki Yamashita's surrender in the Philippines and she was the first non-Japanese woman to enter Japan after the War, as well as attended the Nuremberg Trials in Germany. She was promoted to Colonel in 1969 and retired in 1970. Postwar, Cochran began flying the new jet aircraft, setting numerous records. She became the first woman pilot to go supersonic. In 1952 at age 47, she tried to challenge the world speed record for women, and tried to borrow an F-86 from the US Air Force but was refused. She then went to the Royal Canadian Air Force and was given a plane and set a new record in 1953 of 1078km/h (670 mph). She became a consultant to Northrop Corporation. She became a close friend of General Dwight Eisenhower. Her friendship turned out to be a major factor in him later deciding to run for president of the United States in 1952, and Jackie played a major role in his successful campaign. God blessed her with more gifts than flying. She was often referred to as the best-looking female in the United States Air Force. Jackie Cochran died on August 9, 1980 at age 74 in Indio, California US.

Phoebe Palmer (539)

Phoebe Worrall was born 18 December 1807 in N. York City. Her father Henry Worrall was a devout Methodist and had experienced a religious conversion during the Wesleyan revival in England before he immigrated to America, her mother was Dorothea Wade Worrall. In 1827 Phoebe married Walter Palmer, a homeopathic physician who was also a serious Methodist. They attended regularly in the Allen Street Methodist Church in New York City, and were interested in the writings of the Founder of Methodism John Wesley and were particularly interested in the Wesley doctrine of Christian perfection, which is the belief that a Christian can live a life free of sin. On 26 July 1837 Phoebe Palmer experienced what John Wesley termed "<u>*entire sanctification*</u>." Other members of her family experienced the same, soon after and they too wanted it for themselves, as well as teach others how to experience that. Phoebe often spoke in Methodist churches, and in camp meetings. Her sister Sarah began having weekly prayer meetings, and within two years Phoebe became the leader of these meetings, which were referred to as the Tuesday meetings for the promotion of Holiness, (we might call them Bible studies or small groups), and were held in Palmer's home, but soon her house had to be enlarged to accommodate them. Beginnings in 1889 men were attending such as bishops, theologians and ministers. Some were Edmund S James, Leonidas Lent Hamline, Jesse T. Peck, and Matthew Simpson. This renewed interest eventually influenced the Methodist Church nationwide; it was not common for women to be in leadership positions. Phoebe and her husband were both leaders in the Holiness meetings and played a significant role in spreading the concept of Christian Holiness throughout the United States and the rest of the world. They produced a monthly magazine <u>*the guide to Holiness*</u> first published in 1864. Phoebe initially edited the magazine until her death. She wrote several books, including <u>*the way to Holiness*</u>, which was a foundational book in the Holiness movement. From the northeastern United States, the movement spread to Canada and the United Kingdom in 1859. In her book <u>*The Promise of the Father*</u> she defended the idea of women in Christian ministry. Phoebe wrote several Hymn Tunes including that of Fanny Crosby's <u>*Blessed Assurance*</u>. Phoebe Palmer has been a key in the rise of <u>The Church of the Nazarene, the Church of God</u>, and <u>the Pentecostal Holiness church</u>. Phoebe Palmer died at age 69 on 2 Nov. 1874, her legacy is the Holiness movement, although it should be noted that churches differ widely on doctrine even within denominations. While Holiness is a Biblical mandate and something every believer should strive for; but this important detail is missing and that is: <u>the fact that absolute holiness is impossible to attain in this life</u>.

Susan Boyle (540)

Susan Magdalane Boyle was born 1 April, 1961 in Scotland. She was raised in the West Lothian area of Scotland. Her father was a miner and veteran of WW-II and sometimes worked as a singer at the Bishop's Blaze, and her mother Bridget was a shorthand typist. Both her parents had Irish links. Susan had a high IQ, and was misdiagnosed with Asperger syndrome (*A type of Autism with generally higher functioning people, poor social interactions, and social skills.*) She was bullied as a child. After leaving school with a few qualifications, she took some government training programs and performed at local venues, took singing lessons from vocal coach Fred O'Neil, and participated in a few singing competitions. I watched her when she first auditioned on *Britain's got talent* singing: '*I Dreamed a Dream*" from Les Miserables in 2009, she had almost abandoned her desire to try that show, but on the urging of Fred O'Neil she went anyway, and it changed her life; with that performance she rose to fame. It was magnificent, bringing the entire audience and the jury to their feet for longer than ever before. She instantly became world famous. I saw *Les Miserables* in London and Susan's performance was better. She released her album in 2009, and it became the UK's best-selling debut album of all time. In her first year of fame Boyle earned in excess of *Five Million British Pounds*. That show was aired to 103 million viewers on 20 different web sites by December 2009 her audition was named the most watched You Tube ever; Her newspaper interview appeared in China, Brazil, and the Middle East. That success was continued with the release of her 2nd album "*The Gift*". She released more in 2011, 2012, 2013, and 2019. In 2012 she performed at Windsor Castle for the Queen's Diamond Jubilee Pageant singing "*Mull of Kintyre*". As of 2021 Boyle has sold more than 19 million records. In her private life Susan is Roman Catholic and supports several charitable causes. She has performed in a duet with one of her musical idols Elaine Page in London in 2009. On 16 September 2010 Boyle sang at the Papal mass performed for Pope Benedict XVI at Bellahouston Academy in Glasgow Scotland in the park to a crowd of 65,000. Although Boyle was not eligible for the 2010 Grammy Award, its host Stephen Colbert paid tribute to Boyle at the ceremony telling the audience about this 48-year-old Scottish lady. In September 2018 Boyle was confirmed to be a contestant in America's got talent. When asked why she joined the competition, she stated that she wanted to win, and performed on 7 January 2019 singing Wild Horses she received a golden buzzer and went on to the finals but did not make the top five. Later she performed in the opening series of the Tokyo Olympics. She became known as the lady who shut up Simon Cowell.

Alphabetical Volume 3

Albert L. Ireland (462)
Alexander Young (485)
Alex Newman (504)
Alfred Vogel (444)
Alice Ball (439)
Anselm of Canterbury (508)
Ariana (438)
Audrey Hepburn (456)
Augustine of Hippo (413)
Betsy Ross (431)
Bob Dole (490)
Brandon Judd (419)
Bruce Olson (488)
Cai Lun (532)
Carlos Ott (493)
Cesar Pelli (412)
Christiane Amanpour (523)
Clark Gable (459)
Condoleezza Rice (436)
C. S. Lewis (519)
David Hume (406)
David Niven (457)
David Warren (468)
David Yonggi Cho (467)
Debra N Lewis (429)
Desiderius Erasmus (434)
D. Howard Hitchcock (489)
Dinesh D'Souza (405)
Elizabeth Freeman (530)
Elizabeth Fry (513)
Eric Metaxas (410)
E. V. Hill (534)
Francis Mills Swanzy (484)
Frank E. Midkiff (478)
Gerrit Cornelis Berkouwer (475)
Glenn Youngkin (536)
Hans Wilsdorf (491)
Harmeet Dhillon (428)

Harry Weinberg (472)
Helio Gracie (401)
Henry L. Deneen (510)
Herman Boerhaave (476)
Hugo Junkers (522)
Immanuel Kant (509)
Irving Copi (411)
Jacqueline Cochran (538)
Jack Webb (500)
James H. Case (454)
Jay Adams (517)
Jessica (Jessi) Combs (529)
Jimmy Stewart (455)
John Bunyan (518)
John Dalton (418)
John Fund (452)
John Gibson Paton (469)
John Owen (520)
Joseph John Gurney (512)
Josh Hawley (427)
Julia Child (416)
Julia Coleman (451)
Karl Barth (474)
Kathy Ireland (424)
Kay Coles James (463)
Keli'i Akina (407)
Kim Potter (502)
Lady Jane Grey (531)
Laura Ingraham (423)
Lawrence B. Jones (403)
Leo Terrell (492)
Lisa Boothe (425)
Lou Holtz (426)
Louisa May Alcott (527)
Louis Marie Cordonnier (516)
Louise (437)
Lowell Smith Dillingham (465)
Mark A. Morgan (421)

Mary Todd Lincoln (524)
Mae Jemison (446)
Margaret (Peggy) Garner (528)
Maria Sharapova (526)
Marie Bashkirtseff (535)
Mark Meadows (435)
Martha Gellhorn (537)
Michael Gangloff (470)
Michele Bachmann (464)
Mike Huckabee (402)
Millard Dean Fuller (415)
Miranda Devine (481)
Mollie Hemingway (443)
Naftali Bennett (495)
Nigel Rowe (503)
Niuta Teitelbaum (499)
Noah Webster (482)
Olga of Kiev aka Helga (497)
Patricia Bath (440)
Paul Newman (458)
Peng Shuai (471)
Pete Anderson (515)
Pete Hegseth (507)
Peter Schweizer (422)
Phoebe palmer (539)
Rachel Campos-Duffy (514)
Renzo Piano (505)
Richard Baxter (521)
Richard R. Kelley (449)
Rick Monday (432)
Robert vernon (409)
Ronald DeSantis (448)
Rosemary Jensen (453)
Ruddy F. Tongg (479)
Rudolf Bultmann (473)
Russell Blaylock (400)
Sabina Oster Wurmbrand (420)
Sarah Huckabee Sanders (450)
Sarah Palin (525)
Sendor Nemeth (466)
Serena Williams (511)
Shirley Temple (461)
Sissel Kyrkjebo (460)
Stanley Kennedy (480)
Steve Hilton (404)

Susan Boyle (540)
Theo H. Davies (483)
Thomas Aquinas (430)
Tim Scott (506)
Tom Catena (433)
Tom De Meester (447)
Trischa Zorn (445)
Victor Davis Hanson (408)
Victor Orban (442)
Willard Metcalf (496)
William H Parker (414)
William Penn (494)
William R. Dunn (533)
William Worrall Mayo (417)
William Wrigley Jr. (486)
Winsome Sears (477)
Yulia Tymoshenko (498
Yvonne Clark (441)

Printed by Libri Plureos GmbH in Hamburg, Germany